Law and Economics in Developing Countries

The Hoover Institution
gratefully acknowledges the
generous support of the

EARHART FOUNDATION

Law and Economics in Developing Countries

Edgardo Buscaglia
William Ratliff

HOOVER INSTITUTION PRESS
STANFORD UNIVERSITY
STANFORD, CALIFORNIA

www.hoover.org

Hoover Institution Press Publication No. 469

First printing, 2002
14   13   12   11   10   09   08   10 9 8 7 6 5 4 3

Manufactured in the United States of America
The paper used in this publication meets the minimum
Requirements of the American National Standard for Information
Sciences—Permanence of Paper for Printed Library Materials,
ANSI Z39.48-1984. ∞

Library of Congress Cataloging-in-Publication Data
    Buscaglia, Edgardo.
    Law and economics in developing countries /
Edgardo Buscaglia and William Ratliff.
        p.   cm.—(Hoover Institution Press publication ; no. 469)
    Includes bibliographical references and index.
    ISBN-10: 0-8179-9772-5 (pbk.: alk. paper)
    ISBN-13: 978-0-8179-9772-4 (pbk.: alk. paper)
    1. Law and economics.   2. Law—Economic aspects—Developing
countries.   I. Ratliff, William E.   II. Title.   III. Series: Hoover
Institution Press ; 469.
K487.E3 B438 2001
330'.09172'4—dc21   00-027213

Contents

Preface

Every day the media reports on the many and varied problems individuals, private firms, and governments encounter in the developing countries and emerging markets in Asia, Africa, and Latin America. Books are published and conferences convened on the "new economic model" of free markets, on the growth of civil societies, and on transitions to democracy in the developing world. Much less attention is given, however, to identifying and designing the legal institutions needed to secure successful market reforms and sustain civil societies. For example, in most developing countries that are undertaking market reforms, it is still expensive and time-consuming to determine property rights. Insecure aspects of property rights include multiple, high, and unanticipated taxes repeatedly applied to the same assets; unclear definitions of terms and unpredictable enforcement of contracts; inconsistent application of property laws complicated by corruption; excessive and unjustified regulatory intervention; and sometimes even confiscations. This lack of institutional predictability and security makes smooth, efficient, economical, and productive social and economic interactions more difficult, thereby hampering investments, savings, market reforms, and economic growth.

During the past ten years law and economics have focused on how laws and legal procedures affect economic growth and development in poor countries. Many scholars have written theoretical studies on the links between a reliable legal system and economic decision making (e.g., Buscaglia, Ratliff, and Cooter 1997), but few have tested their policy recommendations using data from actual reform experiences. We fill part of that vacuum by focusing on public policy reforms in the legal and judicial domains, particularly on changes affecting the private sector and its relations with the government. Without effective reforms in these areas, political and market reforms will remain incomplete and insecure. This book is the first to incorporate extensive lessons learned from actual efforts to implement reforms in selected countries in Africa, Asia, Eastern Europe, and Latin America.

We begin by examining the substantive and procedural legal factors that developing nations need to promote political stability and economic growth. We then identify the legal reforms that foster economic efficiency and political stability, such as formalizing local norms and practices and transplanting and integrating international legal norms. We also examine the political and economic impact of laws as they are applied and enforced—or not applied and enforced—by court systems and alternative dispute resolution mechanisms. Developing countries must implement legal and judicial reforms; without them, economic reforms that give power to the private sector cannot be considered "market" reforms. Finally, we describe how the corruption, inefficiency, and ineffectiveness of dysfunctional courts affect economic development and the legitimacy of the political systems in developing countries.

In this book we hope to deepen the interest of both informed general readers and students of law and economics by identifying and promoting constructive public policies in developing countries. On the basis of our experience in the field, we recommend legal and judicial reforms that have been shown to promote economic development. These policies recognize and develop the links between laws, legal procedures, and economic well-being. After extensive work in the field, we have come to recognize that the true actors in these reforms are the lawyers, social scientists, and others in developing countries who propose and implement the policies that make lives easier and more rewarding for their people.

The book is divided into two parts, with a number of case studies to illustrate major points. An introduction explains how the law and economics of development enables one to better understand the impact of laws and legal procedures on economic behavior in developing countries. A conclusion connects the matters studied in the book and draws general recommendations from them. It suggests what needs to be studied in the years ahead.

In the first part we focus on the links between norms (i.e., substantive law) and economic efficiency. Chapter 1 identifies the sources of laws that most enhance economic growth under different conditions and includes a case study on the causes and evolution of intellectual property rights in Latin America. Chapter 2 explores the international aspects of linking economic development and legal reforms, with a case study of the history of Latin American legal and economic integration.

In the second part we show how the application and enforcement of law (procedures) affects economic behavior. Chapter 3 describes and analyzes the economic impact of the judiciary in developing countries and includes an empirical analysis of judiciaries in Latin America to show how legal and economic factors can be used to reform the courts. Chapter 4 examines the role of such alternative dispute resolution (ADR) mechanisms as mediation and arbitration and their impact on the costs of resolving disputes and reducing uncertainty in economic interactions. Chapter 5, an economic analysis of corrupt behavior in public sectors of developing countries, shows why endemic official corruption is one of the main barriers to economic development. The chapter includes a case study of corruption within Chilean and Ecuadorian courts and proposes measures to combat such corruption.

This book owes its existence to many people who over the years were generous with their time, ideas, and suggestions. They include Gladys Alvarez (judge, president of the Federal Appellate Civil Court, Argentina); Jurgen Backhaus (University of Limburg, Maastricht, The Netherlands); Boudewijn Bouckaert (Universiteit Gent, Belgium); Robert Cooter (University of California at Berkeley Law School); Maria Dakolias (World Bank); Gerrit De Geest (Universiteit Gent, Belgium); Pilar Domingo (Oxford University);

Jose Luis Guerrero (Georgetown University); Elena Highton (judge, Federal Appellate Civil Court, Argentina); Clarisa Long (American Enterprise Institute and Harvard University); Santos Pastor (Universidad Complutense de Madrid, Spain); Thomas Ulen (University of Illinois at Urbana-Champaign College of Law); and Hernando de Soto (Instituto de Libertad y Democracia, Lima, Peru). We would also like to thank Brian Johnson, Shawn McMahon, Megan Miller, Anthony Di Pietro, Cecilia Rivas, and Paulina Sierra-Samano for their valuable research assistance.

Finally, we wish to thank Hoover Institution director John Raisian for encouraging and supporting our work and Patricia Baker, Ann Wood, and Marshall Blanchard of the Hoover Institution Press for putting it in its final form.

Introduction to Law, Governance, and Economic Development

THE CONTEXT AND METHODOLOGY OF LAW AND ECONOMICS

To determine the relationship between law, governance, and economic development, we will pose and answer many questions from the perspectives of economics, politics, and the law. How can a country improve the quality of services provided by its legal/judicial institutions? How should governments reform their legal systems and judiciaries to promote economic growth and social development? Which legal institutions should be reformed first? What new institutions must be created? What new laws must be introduced and in what order? What precedents or models will enhance efficiency and equity? What main economic roles should the judiciary play in a modern market economy?

A new consensus, which emerged during the 1990s in most of the developing world, is founded on the massive evidence that state-sponsored models of economic development have given poor results in the short and long terms. Reacting to the statist failures of the past, the current paradigm gives private sectors in developing countries a more active and powerful role. The state is perceived to be in urgent need of improving its institutional capacity to facilitate the participation of the private sector in economic development (World Bank 1997).

1

The import substitution approach to industrialization has been incapable of generating a stock of capital sufficient to launch poor countries into economic growth (Packenham 1995; Buscaglia, Ratliff, and Cooter 1997). The political and social failures of command-and-control social experiments could no longer be denied. Governments in most parts of the non-Asian developing world that were unable to supply such basic public goods as health and education began embracing market reforms as the only alternative, at first hardly realizing that market systems involve much more than giving the private sector the power to allocate resources. Most of the legal and judicial frameworks in developing countries then and many today reflect a past reality that has not adapted to modern organizational and technological innovations. New forms of corporate structure and intellectual property are not even recognized in many developing countries' legal frameworks (Buscaglia and Long 1997). Only after implementing some economic reforms did most governments in the Western world begin to realize that a private sector–led approach to economic development requires, among other things, a compatible set of legal institutions. For example, not until Argentina had privatized most of the state-owned enterprises did it question the legal environment that resulted in a lack of competition and serious market abuse after privatization (Ratliff and Fontaine 1990, 1993). Today, legal reforms are being considered or are in some degree under way around the developing world, though they still lag far behind economic reforms. Even Asian countries, which in some cases engineered economic growth with limited recourse to law (Winn 1994), are now building and/or reforming legal frameworks. Some parts of the developing world may now be on the verge of the legal revolution envisioned by Adam Smith more than two hundred years ago.

Coase (1960) has shown that market transaction costs determine the nature and organization of economic activities. Key factors determining the performance of public and private organizations are (1) the internal rules and hierarchies in the organization and (2) the legal and market-related external institutional environment. Economic and political reforms in many parts of the developing world during the 1990s have convinced reformers that constructive development requires newly designed organizations that are able to harmonize the creation of private wealth and the progress of society in general. It is important for laws to serve the interests of both the institutions that apply them and the society at large. In fact, the remarkable degree to which some Asian countries in the post–World War II period grew and shared that growth with most sectors of society was generally due to their success in developing just such regulations and institutions (Root 1996). Most countries in Latin America and other regions did not even begin moving toward Asian-level productivity until the 1990s. In many countries continuing low labor productivity, unevenly shared growth, and corruption—the transfer of wealth for private benefit by the use of public office—can be explained in large part by culture and institutions. Stated differently, the countries lack convictions and institutions to promote an overlapping of public and private interests (Harrison 1997, 1985; North 1990; Ratliff 1999). The challenge today in the developing world is twofold: (1) to redesign public and private organizations, and reform norms and procedures, so that individuals and organizations will benefit by economic and political development of the society generally and (2) to make it expensive for those who choose to operate outside this framework.

For a long time the impact of private law (e.g., property, contract, or tort laws) and public law (e.g., constitutional law) on organizational behavior in developing countries was not explored. Several recent analyses (Trebilcock 1997; World Bank 1997; Campos and Root 1996), however, examine the quality of public sector governance and its relationship to the economic progress of nations. These studies cover the relationship between political systems, institutions, and economic performance. They go far toward answering two important questions: (1) What types of institutions are most conducive to economic development? and (2) What factors or conditions encourage or impede the adoption of institutions enhancing economic efficiency?

As Orr and Ulen (1993) argue, "A government that credibly commits itself to upholding rights of property and contract enforcement not only provides a basis whereby partners in economic transactions can trust each other, it also reinforces the hope that the government itself can be trusted to transact honorably and to meet its contractual obligations." But in most developing countries the costs for determining property rights are still high, when they are possible at all.

Hernando de Soto (1997, 1989) has conducted a detailed original examination of property rights in developing countries, particularly Peru. His analysis provides answers to key questions using the economic theory of property. First, de Soto asks what should be privately owned in an environment where state ownership has been the norm until recently and, second, how should property rights be assigned and enforced to assure that social norms regarding property will be expressed in the written law. He reports that in Peru, and seemingly in most parts of the Third World, formalized land titles exist for less than 10 percent of rural property and half of urban property. He shows how the lack of predictable property rights affects the behavior of private firms, investments, and economic growth. Unanticipated, multiple, and high taxation applied to the same bundle of property rights again and again hampers the formalization of land titles. De Soto's analysis demonstrates the decisive link between the security of private ownership and the growth of market transactions. The unclear definition of contractual obligations, inconsistent application of the laws coupled with corruption, and ad hoc regulations leave property rights insecure and increase transaction costs within the marketplace. This institutional instability hampers investments, savings, and the consumption of durable goods. De Soto shows that compatibility between social norms and written law assures that the law will be followed by the average citizen; he stresses the fact that, in the absence of clear and enforceable legal rules, people will substitute clear and enforceable customs and norms. As stated in Ratliff and Buscaglia (1997), from an economic standpoint, state-sponsored systems of legal rules detached from customs may not be as efficient as an enforced set of legal rules deriving from the community itself; the tendency to centralize has been felt almost everywhere (Meese 1999). Peru's experience attests to the high transaction costs of a state-sponsored or centralized property registry that ignores the uses and customs prevailing in agricultural land tenure, particularly with respect to individual land plots.

In Douglass North's tradition, markets can be considered institutional mechanisms (i.e., interrelated systems of behavioral rules) within which rights and obligations are exchanged by participants. Changes are needed in the legal and judicial frameworks of developing countries before economic reforms that give power to the private sector can be truly considered "market" reforms. A market-compatible legal system requires answering such questions as (1) To what degree does law promote economic development? (2) To what extent is economic development affected if rules are clearly defined, public and consistently applied, or the reverse? (3) How are investment projects affected by mechanisms to resolve conflicts based on the binding decisions of an independent judiciary and fair procedures?

Examples of the great flexibility that the legal and judicial systems need to adapt a nation's laws to a dynamic economic system are abundant. Broadly speaking, legal and judicial systems in a market economy must (1) establish the standard rules of socioeconomic interaction, (2) set the rules of interaction between the public and the private sectors, (3) enforce these rules through the courts, and (4) resolve conflicts among individuals and groups. More specifically, a modern market economy needs laws to (1) define rights and market relationships when new forms of corporate structure emerge, (2) provide decisions on contractual obligations that can be extended to new forms of financial instruments as well as tangible and intangible property, and (3) define and enforce the rights of victims of new technologies while protecting the environment from newly emerging risks. The formation of larger markets and the possibility of longer term contracts, both necessary conditions for economic growth, are hampered by an unclear or undefined system of legal rules and by the inconsistent interpretation and application of those rules. As Cooter (1996, 2–3) states in a pioneering piece, "If economic law is poorly adapted to the economy, expectations conflict, cooperating is difficult, and disputes consume resources. Conversely, if economic law is adapted to the economy, people cooperate with each other, harmonize their expectations, and use resources efficiently and creatively." That is,

if public institutions are defective and political conditions too un-
stable, private contractual arrangements will become riskier and
negatively affect private investment. Finally, giving citizens greater
security and involvement in the future of their country "reduces
the long-term danger that social movements will contest regime legitimacy and topple the government, which, in turn, induces
longer time horizons in the investment calculations of the private
sector, an important determinant of sustainable development"
(Root, Ratliff, and Morgan 1999).

The process of economic transformation in developing countries—by means of deregulation, the privatization of the means of
production, and expanding international trade in complex goods
and services—needs an effective legal framework with clear rules
for economic interaction. For example, there are often increasingly
complicated contractual relationships among savers, producers, investors, and customers. These relationships need a system of rules
to enhance risk management. Thus legal, judicial, and alternative
dispute resolution systems are essential to a society with increasingly higher social complexities and risks generated by individual
and group interactions. The clear identification of these needs, and
the discovery of improved mechanisms for dealing with them, is
the first problem to be solved by the economic analysis of law in
developing countries.

In most developing countries, uncertainty related to the application of the law—due to discretionary power and the inefficient
administration of justice—is increasing transaction costs and fostering corruption. Lowering of business transaction costs and the
eradication of endemic corruption require public policies that are
based on empirical studies. Some recent studies by Cooter and
Ginsberg (1996), Buscaglia and Guerrero (1995), and Mauro
(1995) add empirical dimensions to the analysis of the economic
impact of the laws in the areas of constitutional rules, laws against
counterfeiting, and anticorruption policies. Law and economics
have much to contribute to the analysis of how institutions fight
these problems and promote economic development. Their comparative advantage over other disciplines is in two areas: (1) they
can pinpoint those legal institutions that are imposing high trans-

action costs on business transactions and (2) they provide ways to empirically identify what types of laws and procedures best promote or impede a competitive economic environment. Extant works in this field cover the analysis of the actual (positive) and desired (normative) links between law and economics. Douglass North (1990) has pointed to the relationship among property rights, transaction costs, and economic growth. The study of market and nonmarket behavior reacting to different legal environments falls within the best tradition of the University of Chicago approach to law and economics. Yet other approaches need to be incorporated into the legal and economic study of development. Among them are the study of what types of organizations emerge under different kinds of economic environments (Williamson 1991) and the analysis of how to best identify those organizations with the potential to hamper economic growth, as described by Mancur Olson (1993, 1982). In short, scholars trying to explain the lack of consistent and steady economic development in developing countries need to understand the impact of laws on markets and on their organizations.

With this and other problems in mind, we will identify the most effective legal and judicial mechanisms to interpret and translate social norms into laws in less-developed countries in such a way that economic growth would be enhanced. That is, we will identify changes in laws, regulations, and enforcement mechanisms that, within the legal tradition of each country, would enhance economic efficiency, improve equity, and promote general development. For example, when a law allows banks to repossess loan-related collateral with a minimum of transaction costs, interest rates charged on those loans will be lower than when the law forces banks to collect over multiple procedural barriers with an unpredictable judiciary. Edmund Kitch (1983) argues that law and economics focus on the impact of legal rules, understood as a system of rewards and penalties, that affect individual behavior. These rewards and penalties are defined by laws, regulations, doctrines, court cases, and social norms, among other things. The chief goal of law and economics as applied to the study of development is to analyze how individuals and firms react to different systems of legal rules in order to identify those laws that would best promote wealth as a consequence. In this sense, the law and economics of development follow a methodology based on understanding how to enhance a more efficient social order through legal reform.

Measuring the extent of the impact of the law on economic development requires more than the already abundant observations and statements of seeming logical truths. It requires empirical inquiry, the new frontier in law and economics. Empirical studies of conditions in individual countries help us determine the norms nations need to address to promote economic growth and development. When legal requirements for economic development have been identified, it is necessary to pinpoint the most suitable sources for the needed laws. For example, a nation may enact laws inspired by domestic social norms and customs, or it may draw laws in part or in whole from international legal transplants. Where countries need to formulate a law, the law and economics of development can shed light on the comparative efficiency of legal transplants versus the adoption of customs and norms as sources of law. Cases abound where simple transplants to developing countries (e.g., of intellectual property laws) have been rejected after the law was enacted by the receiving political institutions in particular and the societies in general. At the same time, law and economics as a discipline should also look at the procedural aspects of the law and their impact on business transactions. To lay the groundwork for fruitful reforms, the symptoms of a dysfunctional court system— one that is inefficient, ineffective, and corrupt—need to be stated and their impact on economic development understood. Only then can reforms be effectively planned and implemented.

CHAPTER 1

The Economic Impact of Legal Norms in Developing Countries

EFFICIENCY AND THE SOURCE OF LEGAL NORMS

It is commonly believed that in a sovereign nation all law-making power is in the hands of the state. But although the state often plays a major role, Mattei (1998) and Greif (1999) have shown that it is wrong to think of the state as all-powerful and, rather, that impersonal exchanges can be well developed without state-enforced legal frameworks. In these cases, community responsibility systems and private sector associations adopt, provide, and enforce rules covering property rights, contracts, systems of civil responsibility (i.e., tort rules), and other matters. These legal rules, sometimes provided and enforced within the nonstate domain, are designed to prevent or resolve problems (i.e., conflicting claims) among market participants. Analysts thus need to understand a nation's source of legal order as the interplay between the public domain, where legal rules are provided by the state, and the private domain, where rules are created by nonstate parties, with the objective of facilitating interactions and reducing transaction costs.

Legal rules in the commercial domain are supposed to cover specific types of transactions within territorial political boundaries. When transactions are transnational, however, the territorial aspect of laws may be problematic. For example, when transactions involve foreign intellectual property—particularly between developed and developing countries—the two legal environments may subject the market participants and patent users to different transactions costs. Therefore, we should consider costs on transnational transactions imposed by differences in legal rules as nontariff barriers to trade. In recent years the traditional approaches or solutions have been to

1.   Allow the parties in an exchange to "choose the law" that would rule the transaction. Under this so-called jurisdictional competition, legal systems compete to be the jurisdiction within which certain transactions are performed.

2.   Achieve intergovernmental cooperation through international treaties (e.g., the Paris Patent Convention or the Madrid Trademark Convention).

3.   Legally harmonize or unify the two legal systems under the same doctrines and enforcement mechanisms (e.g., European Union).

4.   Transplant the law from the country with lower transaction costs to the country with higher transaction costs.

All these solutions overcome the problem of territoriality by creating a legal and institutional environment for international transactions that treats them as if they were national transactions.

The political and economic costs and benefits associated with each solution may differ. The "choice of law" approach generally assumes that the legal options are equivalent in complexity and sophistication. But the original designs of supranational legal institutions, including the European Community (now Union), the Common Market of the South (Mercosur), and the North American Free Trade Agreement (NAFTA), require special conditions for harmonization and/or legal unification. These conditions include the presence of supranational issues (costs and benefits) affecting two or more countries that could not be addressed by individual countries, among them international pollution, immigration, communication infrastructure, and regional international trade cooperation within the world economy.

A market for any good or service is conceived of as an institutional environment within which rights and obligations to the assets exchanged are defined and enforced according to generally accepted rules. In the process of overcoming the territoriality problem through any of the four solutions mentioned above, the parties are at the same time expanding the size of the market to a foreign jurisdiction. For example, the justification for legal harmonization is reducing transaction costs through economies of scale. In contrast, jurisdictional competition allows the private parties performing transactions to discover which legal system may better serve their goals.

One recent line of research in the law and economics of development literature compares the economic impact of the different sources of legal norms, such as laws enacted by Congress, executive branch decrees, judge-made legal interpretations through sentencings, and scholarly articles. In their early exploration of this topic, Cooter (1996) and Buscaglia (1993) argue that efficiency is enhanced by a "bottom-up" process of capturing society's norms—as rules of behavior that facilitate social interaction—that in human interaction are the main substantive source for enacting laws.

This decentralized and spontaneous approach to lawmaking is in sharp contrast to the centralization proposed by the first law and development movement that during the 1960s and 1970s proposed a "modernization" of developing countries' laws through transplants enacted by centralized political bodies. The most important works in this first movement—Seidman (1978), Galanter (1974), and Trubek (1972)—supported comprehensive, centralized, and top-down legislative reform aimed at modernizing the public and private dimensions of the law.

This top-down approach to lawmaking served the purposes of a centralized and interventionist state looking to import substitution to bring development. From the early 1930s until the late 1980s, almost all developing countries encouraged domestic (import substitution) manufacturing investment, suppressed agricultural prices, and expanded their public sector enterprises while attempting to stimulate savings and investment through taxation and credit. A shortage of domestic physical capital was seen as the key impediment to development. Import substitution industries grew behind protective walls based on subsidies and tariffs in a milieu where policymakers ignored many other determinants of the rate of economic growth, such as investment in human capital. Protecting import substitution industries allowed domestic prices and costs to far exceed international prices and created little incentive for efficiency. These protected industries produced substitutes for imports but were dependent on the import of raw materials and technology. Import demand by these industries grew rapidly as these firms imported capital goods to accelerate investment. The antiexport bias, combined with the import substitution program, caused a scarcity of foreign exchange; this, in turn, created a structural barrier to investment in expensive first-rate technologies. Within this environment, protected from international trade, firms continued investing in second-rate technologies. This approach to development ended with the international debt crisis of the 1980s, when developing countries' policymakers realized that internal markets and import substitution could not bring sustainable growth, followed by the collapse of state-dominated economies all over the world in the 1990s. But during the decades of import substitution, the necessary high level of public sector intervention could only be legally sustained through a top-down centralized lawmaking approach such as the one proposed by the law and development movement at that time.

Within the four legal traditions that are generally recognized in the twentieth century (i.e., civil law; common or judge-made law, as found in those countries following the English tradition; administrative law; and socialist law), Eastern Europe and China have slowly shifted from a socialist legal system characterized by centralized public rules toward a prerevolutionary private civil law strongly influenced by the codified legal systems of France and Germany. In all these traditions, regional and local laws have suffered from expanded centralized administrative laws that regulate the relationship between the state and the private sector. As Mattei (1997, 74) states, "The law was equated with the legal production of the state. Consequently, in its understanding, the law exists only as a function of the enforcement mechanisms behind it." Under these circumstances, administrative law and civil codes, as the frameworks establishing the rules to be followed by the state and private individuals, have been the by-product of the expansion and intrusion of government throughout Western societies.

In reality, however, daily interactions among people and businesses are often guided by widely accepted informal rules; these rules are often applied when mediation or arbitration is used to resolve conflicts. Only when these informal but prevailing rules of behavior are captured by formal legislation will a law actually promote the greatest possible efficiency. Laws that try to impose and enforce behavioral patterns that are foreign to a market or region tend to increase friction and production and transaction costs. Thus, one important challenge facing developing countries in their current legal evolution is choosing between centralized and decentralized lawmaking capabilities. In national legal systems of civil law, where parliaments enjoy a power advantage in legislative production, developing countries face a critical choice. They can attempt social engineering either by creating regulations in a centralized top-down manner or by legally formalizing social norms and enforcing them in a bottom-up approach. Cooter (1996) believes that the ineffectiveness of the laws enacted by parliaments in many countries today reflect the lack of links between the essence of what the law stipulates and the social norms followed by businesses and people in their daily activities and lives. When regulations or laws lack this compatibility, the costs of complying and enforcing them becomes higher. These are the so-called bad laws mentioned by de Soto in his path-breaking book (1989), in which he demonstrates the far higher transaction costs of complying with the formal law in comparison to following the social norm within an informal market. In de Soto's work these higher transaction costs are rooted in the drive of governments to centralize lawmaking without regard to the people's actual social practices.

Only when laws and regulations reflect the practices of the people will the transaction costs of social interactions decline and a tendency toward efficiency occur. From de Soto's (1997) perspective, the size of many informal sectors around the globe is intimately related to the way laws and regulations fail to capture social practices. Following Hayek (1973), we believe that market participants' need for information derives from added social complexity and requires public policy to decentralize lawmaking by capturing local norms and thus reducing market transaction costs. Buscaglia and Ratliff

(1997) and Cooter (1996b, 148) believe that "efficiency requires the enforcement of customs in business communities to become more important relative to the regulation of business."

Following the pioneering studies by Cooter (1996, 1994), Mattei (1996), and Buscaglia (1993), we argue that the laws generating voluntary compliance are those that are truly compatible with the ethical code prevailing in a society. Individuals seek the kind of predictability they think will increase their capacity to generate wealth. This "grab what you can" approach is not a priori desirable or compatible with long-term survival (Buscaglia 1993). Whatever the level and concentration of political and economic power, the social norms and values that underpin the prevailing and predictable rules of political and economic interaction in a society enhance the efficiency of conducting business by reducing the transaction costs of interacting in the marketplace. These norms within society must be discovered and transformed into formalized legal rights and obligations.

To extend Cooter's (1996) analysis, in order to enhance efficiency, politics must follow not just the market but also the nonmarket social norms (Buscaglia 1993). In a more comprehensive fashion, society's market and nonmarket rules for social interaction provide a lawmaking guide for the legislature and the judiciary. By making laws that are comprehensible to ordinary citizens, the transaction costs of human interactions decrease and allow society to achieve efficiency in its market and nonmarket activities. The evolution of intellectual property laws in developing countries, described later in this chapter, is an example of how legal transplants offer a channel through which national laws begin to represent business practices and social norms.

LEGAL TRANSPLANTS, POLITICAL CULTURE, AND ECONOMIC EFFICIENCY

Countries have many choices when looking for models of laws to adopt. Transplants and other levels of influence can go in any direction. For example, variations of U.S. criminal law have been adopted in Western Europe (Nadelmann 1993). Deng Xiaoping, no doubt thinking mainly of Taiwan, envisioned that the "one country, two systems" formula worked out with Great Britain for Hong Kong is "an example for other nations in settling disputes history has bequeathed to them" (Deng 1993, 14). Most transplants today, however, go from developed to developing countries, and those are our focus here. A country can adopt or write a law based on the work of its own institutions—parliament, executive, judiciary, or academy. Or it can transplant a legal norm from outside its borders. If a country chooses the transplant route, which of many alternatives should it choose? Analysts have not yet concluded which of these alternatives in which cases best serves the needs of a country that wants to develop efficiently and equitably.

Watson (1978) has shown that in the past most legal reforms have been transplants, but his research and conclusions have raised new questions. Does Watson's analysis speak to the importance and impact of transplants worldwide (i.e., even in China?) or only to the Western countries he examined (Alford 1995)? Why did some countries opt for civil law as opposed to common law, the separation of powers as opposed to parliamentary systems, or vice versa? Why, with such a vast international pool of laws to choose from, were some rules and institutions chosen by so many while others were generally rejected? For much of the twentieth century, the question was why half the world "chose" to live under socialist law? More recently, the questions have become why so many countries adopt the same rules to protect intellectual property, enforce competition laws, or even compensate victims of accidents? As Mattei (1994) pointed out, one reason could be "prestige," a variable that cannot be measured or verified. Prestige is tied closely to another form of influence: politics and ideology, often in the guise of economics. The two prominent twentieth century examples in what is now the developing world were dependency and communism, political ideologies that carried with them the most counterproductive of economic agendas. As Packenham (1992, 41) wrote of dependency, it was dishonest in that it was "unfalsifiable." That is, in its own terms it cannot be proven wrong because it does not "specify or imply types of data that would disconfirm" it (Ratliff 1989–90). In the end, of course, reality overwhelmed the dependency supporters and Communists through massive economic collapse or stagnation. But frustration with economic developments under any economic system can lead to the adoption of economically counterproductive policies. Political expediency also can lead to the implementation of bad—or sometimes good—economic policies (de Soto 1997; Ratliff 1999).

Today, with the wreckage of command economies piled high around us, market reformers are asking more practical questions and conducting cost-benefit analyses to determine which legal rules and systems are most efficient, productive, and equitable. These analyses can often yield instructive results, but they too have complications. Broadly speaking, policies and results may be different because the important variables vary from time to time, from place to place, from reformer to reformer. For example, whereas regulations to support governance for equitable growth have been of great importance for decades in parts of Asia, they are not nearly as important in Latin America and other developing regions (Ratliff 1999). Legal—and other—reforms may also be threatened by interest groups, from the Communist Party in China to the National Congress in Brazil, all of which may have much to lose, at least in the short term, by any major change in a legal system from which they have benefited in the past (Lam 1999). At the same time, the successful implementation of any reform depends on those agents, often interest groups, who are responsible for introducing the reforms and ultimately for their effective enforcement (Buscaglia, Ratliff, and Dakolias, 1995). When effective enforcement is missing (Alford 1995), reforms may stall or move slowly.

Other scholars have studied the sequencing of reforms, that is, gradualism versus radical (i.e., "big-bang") approaches to economic reforms in Latin America (Martinelli and Tommasi 1997). Given the fact that economic reforms ought to go hand in hand with legal reforms, the analysis in this book can be used to understand the pros and cons of radical reform. A comprehensive reform package allows for an increased accumulation of political support in the short run in two differing ways. On the one hand, radical reforms based on comprehensive packages may allow each interest groups' losses in one area to be compensated by gains in some other area, thereby increasing the probability of this group's support. On the other hand, comprehensive reforms may be designed to draw strong support from frustrated and disenfranchised sectors and allow a government to divide, curtail, or crush some large interest groups within the country.

In countries in which comprehensive legal reforms were proposed or undertaken—such as Argentina, Hungary, and the Czech Republic—business sectors associated with foreign investment supported legal and judicial reforms in areas clearly associated with their commercial activities. This occurred as the spread of democratic systems and the emergence of economic blocs reduced the opportunities for unpredictable and discretionary government behavior. Also, technological developments expanded the size of the markets of most goods and services while increasing the speed of the flow of financial resources. In this new context, developing countries' economic policies tended to converge in an unprecedented manner toward the "best-practice" standards demanded by international investors. Investors in Latin America and Eastern Europe demand well-specified clauses in foreign investment laws (World Bank 1997). The reforms represent a package of rules dealing with taxation, trade, companies, bankruptcy, finances, intellectual property, and competition that transplanted best-practice laws adapted to the indigenous conditions through political debate and partial redrafting. For example, the latest company laws in Russia and Argentina, inspired by Western European and American laws, respectively, are cases in point. But in both cases the laws provide for a much higher level of self-enforcement outside state action than is present in the countries from which the laws were taken. The greater level of self-enforcement through local adaptation of legal transplants includes more strict and legally mandated monitoring of the firms' managers by shareholders. These mechanisms tend to minimize the risks of managers' running amok in environments where the court systems are in varying degrees dysfunctional.

Additionally, institutions responsible for producing and distributing market information are currently being introduced and/or revamped in most developing countries (Buscaglia 1996). These watchdog institutions include credit-rating agencies, securities commissions, regulators, company and property registries, the private bar, and "white-collar crime" monitoring groups. All can play an important role in the course of market and private sector development even in cases where property rights are well defined. In undeveloped markets, the rules of market interaction may not be understood well by participants and knowledge of the business environment limited. Engaged parties do not know some important facts in advance, ranging from the reputation of a potential associate to the entire range of details related to business opportunities. Coordination among market participants in complex transactions (e.g., a firm's takeover) is often difficult because potential or actual parties to transactions may not be willing to share all relevant information. In many cases, watchdog institutions are able to increase the availability of market information related to product quality and professional reputation, making it possible to reduce transaction costs through self-enforcement. Since 1990, governments and nongovernmental organizations in Latin America (exclusive of Cuba) have undertaken varying kinds of joint measures to increase the levels of activity of these watch-dog institutions (Buscaglia 1996). In this context, legal reforms ratifying the existence of these self-enforcement mechanisms have had a positive impact on economic transactions by formalizing the norms of business interactions.

To sum up, reforms in most developing countries must confront enormous political and cultural obstacles to real change. In many cases these are manifested in the scourge of corruption, discussed below. More broadly, these are challenges noted by Montesquieu, South America's nineteenth century liberators Simón Bolívar and Francisco de Miranda, Alexis de Tocqueville, Max Weber, Carlos Rangel, Robert Putnam, Samuel Huntington, Mario Vargas Llosa, and many others. Mexico's Nobel Prize–winning Octavio Paz focused his critique on the impact of the three central institutions of Latin American civilization—the church, military, and government—by writing, "Though Spanish-American civilization is to be admired on many counts, it reminds one of a structure of great solidity—at once convent, fortress, and palace—built to last, not to change. In the long run, that construction became a confine, a prison" (Paz 1994, 78). Concluding a study of legal reform on the other side of the world, Alford (1995, 119) writes, "The most important factor in explaining the late appearance and relative insignificance of the idea of intellectual property in the Chinese world lies in what, for a lack of a better term, we might describe as its political culture." Alford continues, "By its very nature, political culture comprises enduring values and practices central to a nation's identity, which foreigners, perforce, should not too readily assume they have either the moral authority or capacity meaningfully to influence" (120).

CASE STUDY: INTELLECTUAL PROPERTY LAWS IN DEVELOPING COUNTRIES

How can the choice of sources of laws have an economic impact on business investment? We will examine intellectual property laws in developing countries in general and in Latin America in particular. In developing countries, the definition and enforcement of clear intellectual property rules are essential for determining the feasibility of investment projects, especially foreign direct investments, and enhancing technological innovation among newly privatized firms. When announcing an intellectual property accord with China in February 1995, the U.S. government (United States Embassy 1995a) defined intellectual property as including computer software, pharmaceuticals, agricultural and chemical products, audiovisual works, books and periodicals, and trademarks. Alford (1995, 1) argues that "intellectually property is defined principally to encompass copyright, patent, and trademark."

The development and commercialization of applied knowledge is widely recognized as the main source of economic growth (Birdzell and Rosenberg 1990). The ability to generate and use new ideas and technologies has always separated the winners from the losers, whether among individuals, firms, or nations. But the views of producers and governments in developing versus technologically advanced nations are very different. Today, the developing countries generally regard the protection of intellectual property as a cultural prejudice and/or an economic policy variable; technologically advanced countries see it as a fundamental right, comparable to the right to physical property. In Latin America, for example, intellectual property generally is regarded not as an asset to be held privately but rather as "the heritage of humanity." In one of the authors' Taiwan-pirated versions of the *Analects*, Confucius speaks of himself as a transmitter and not a creator of knowledge (Confucius B.C. 1923). Alford (1996, 29, 17) notes that in China "true scholars wrote for edification and moral renewal rather than profit," adding that "virtually all known examples of efforts by the state to provide protection for what we now term intellectual property in China prior to the twentieth century seem to have been directed overwhelmingly toward sustaining imperial power." In contrast, developed countries enact rules and design institutions to handle problems related to the assertion of private claims to intangible assets, gaps in ownership rights, swift registration of the rights, and easily accessible mechanisms for dispute resolution (Orr and Ulen 1993). Today, the more developed the market economy is, particularly in information-intensive ways, the more important the intellectual property rights framework has to be to promote innovation and efficiency.

Before continuing with our discussion of the campaign against violations of intellectual property by "pirates" in the developing world, we must make a few contextual comments. When the currently developed countries were themselves underdeveloped, they were not nearly as concerned about intellectual property rights (Alford 1995). An example of the American violation of author's rights was the pirating by theater groups of Gilbert and Sullivan's *H.M.S. Pinafore* in the late 1870s, which led the two British gentlemen to entitle their next operetta *The Pirates of Penzance*. In 1997 estimated piracy rates for computer software alone were substantially higher in developing—China (96 percent of applications pirated), Bulgaria (93 percent), El Salvador and Russia (89 percent)—than developed countries. The dollar loss because of Chinese piracy of software in 1997 is estimated at more than US$ 1.4 billion (Business Software Alliance 1998). The U.S. International Trade Commission claims that foreign violations of

U.S. intellectual property cost the United States up to US$ 61 billion in lost profits annually (Alford 1995). But several "howevers" are in order here before we proceed. Note that these kinds of figures can be misleading because they assume that if cheap pirated versions of the product had not been available to the Chinese, for example, those who have pirated applications would have bought the same product at the established price, which is patently untrue. Most lost "sales" never would have taken place. What is more, despite stricter laws in the developed world—more strict in some countries than others—many software users there also pirate what they use: United States (27 percent of software applications in use), Japan (32 percent), Germany (33 percent), and France (44 percent). The dollar losses to software pirates in the United States in 1997 were estimated at nearly US$ 2.8 billion, twice the figure for China, and many of the U.S. "losses" were in fact lost sales. U.S. dollar losses to pirates in Japan are an estimated 750 million and in Germany more than 500 million (Business Software Alliance 1998).

Conflicts arise when individuals and firms use the intellectual property for financial gain without the permission of the innovator or owner. The United States loses an estimated $3.45 billion annually due to inadequate enforcement of intellectual property rights in information-intensive sectors—such as pharmaceuticals, entertainment software, and motion pictures—in Latin America alone (see table 1).

Primo Braga (1990) observes that governments in developing countries only partially apply or enforce modern intellectual property rules, even when the benefits of such rules are widely recognized by local business interests and by the countries generating the essential technologies. The reasons for the recent emergence of intellectual property reform in developing countries, however, and the complications surrounding it, have not received enough attention because of a failure to recognize how the costs and benefits of legal reform operate on those responsible for enacting the legal reform and how these mesh with differing institutions and cultures. More specifically, in many cases politicians in developing countries see legal reform as a short-term liability that damages their relations with their local constituencies. The benefits of defining

TABLE 1
ESTIMATES OF U.S. LOSSES TO INFRINGEMENT AND COUNTERFEITING IN LATIN AMERICA

Total losses by sector	(in millions of dollars)
Pharmaceuticals	$1,686.0
Business software	1,141.5
Entertainment (not business) software	259.1
Motion pictures	174.0
Music	115.5
Books	70.5
Total	3,446.6

SOURCES: Jeb Blount, "Hands of Steal," *Latin Trade*, November 1996, pp. 50, 52; Business Software Alliance, "1995 BSA/SPA Piracy Study Prepared by International Planning and Research," 18 December 1996.

and enforcing intellectual property rights, in contrast, are seen as more distant and less tangible and thus easily set aside by politicians with their minds on cultivating allies for the next election. This perspective is reinforced by the fact that only 1 percent of worldwide royalties today are generated by residents of less-developed countries (Primo Braga 1990; United States Embassy 1995b). In fact, China and some other countries demonstrate how even some major "outside" influences (e.g., overseas Chinese) may not be "conducive to the elevation" of "legal consciousness" (Lubman 1996b, 1999).

Legal reforms in emerging markets such as Argentina, Brazil, and China are the result of both foreign economic pressures and domestic political conditions; as in China, foreign investment regimes are often "as much a product of incremental and ad hoc responses to challenges" as "an expression of coherent doctrine" (Potter 1986, 174; Buscaglia 1994). These two forces explain the recent international legal convergence in the principles sustaining intellectual property laws. The foreign economic pressures to reform intellectual property laws arise because an increasing proportion of imports into developing countries consists of information-intensive goods and services such as software and products generated through biotechnologies (Buscaglia 1994). The intellectual property contained in these products is more subject to infringements than the simpler labor-intensive exports from developing countries. Understandably, firms generating these technologies in advanced countries have demanded that their governments penalize the unauthorized use of their intellectual property in less-developed countries through trade sanctions or threats to withdraw broader trade benefits. Developing countries that have stagnated for decades under import substitution economics, described earlier, now find themselves retarded in areas necessary for national development. As a result of the aforementioned foreign and domestic pressures, countries such as Argentina, Mexico, Brazil, China, and South Korea were forced to reconsider many of their legal institutions, including their national intellectual property laws, and move toward the legal frameworks prevailing in nations generating standard advanced technologies. For example, the privatization of state monopolies and the shift toward import competition that has taken place in emerging markets (e.g., Argentina, Hungary, and Uganda) produced a vast increase in the demand for high-technology products sold by the industrialized countries. There was a substantial increase in exports of telecommunication and information technology between 1988 and 1993 from the United States (215 percent), Japan (187 percent), and the European Union (97 percent) to developing countries (Buscaglia and Long 1997). This vast increase in international transactions involving information-intensive goods and services (e.g., software) made it necessary to reformulate the legal foundation of intellectual property with twin objectives: to define and enforce the rights of businesses generating high technology and to assure the diffusion of know-how to those countries with the capacity to absorb it. It soon became clear that the international harmonization of intellectual property rules was a sine qua non for the transfer of complex technologies to the developing world. Buscaglia and Long (1997) apply this implicit cost-benefit approach to legal transplants with respect to the recent adoption of intellectual property laws under the World Trade Organization (WTO) umbrella. In short, reconsidering the legal foundation of intellectual property rights was compelled by the increasing permeability of national frontiers and the demand for high-tech products.

The Paris and Berne international conventions signed by most countries in the nineteenth century provided a legal framework for more than a hundred years (Buscaglia and Long 1997). The two main doctrines or legal principles of the conventions were (1) "territoriality," which stated that property rights would be honored according to each state's rules, and (2) "independence," which established that the granting of property rights by one state did not require other states to grant the same rights. These two doctrines, however, have become irrelevant in the new order emerging after the Uruguay Round of talks of the General Agreement on Trade and Tariffs (GATT), the forerunner to the WTO. Under the supervision of the newly founded WTO, harmony or uniformity of laws has been sought to encourage the international flow of goods and services. This new framework has supported granting innovators intellectual property rights—such as patents—and compensation by users for their products based on the business norms of the marketplace. That is, innovators receive compensation from their investments and products so that society more broadly will be able to benefit from the use of innovation that would otherwise have been kept secret.

The international enforcement of intellectual property rights has evolved impressively during the past three decades. For more than a century, the international intellectual property regime of the Paris and Berne conventions provided ample scope for cooperation but left to national legislation the responsibility to define the main aspects of intellectual property rights. After World War II, the balance between the rights of the inventor and the benefits of diffusing technology to less-developed countries became a greater concern. For developing countries, the need for rapid industrialization and fast and vast improvements in technologies justified imposing limitations on the rights and benefits of innovators. In general, developing countries took this route under two circumstances: First, when a patent could only be granted if the intellectual property was worked and exploited within the national frontiers of a country (i.e., a working requirement), and second, when the terms and royalties for licenses of intellectual property could be determined by the government in the absence of agreement by the innovator (i.e., compulsory licensing). Under these circumstances, developing governments abandoned the exchange of benefits between innovator and user and replaced it with an approach based on granting intellectual property rights in exchange for foreign direct investment.

But difficult problems remained. Legal systems in many developing countries are characterized by inconsistent coverage, uncertain terms of protection, arbitrary transferability, compulsory licensing regimes, and inadequate enforcement. As a result, businesses and governments in developed countries concluded they could not afford to invest more and more in knowledge-intensive products and then (effectively) give their product away to other countries however much they needed it. They did not, after all, give it away to people in their own countries who came to need it as well and had provided the conditions and, directly or indirectly, the financing that made the innovations possible. Thus, the need for legal reform was heightened in particular by the technological breakthroughs of the 1970s in the microelectronics, biological inventions, computer software, and other high-technology, knowledge-intensive sectors.

As stated above, intellectual property rights encourage innovators to make their product available in exchange for some form of remuneration. These rights facilitate the transfer of technology from developed to developing countries. The most common means of legally transferring technology is through licensing, in which the holder of the intellectual property rights allows another person or entity to use those rights in exchange for a royalty payment.

Because much intellectual property is produced only after considerable financial investment, the actual, perceived, and expected losses on the part of U.S. firms due to inadequate intellectual property protection influence the willingness of firms to transfer technology to developing countries. In the past, the value of most exports was based on its physical manifestations (e.g., steel), but in recent years, and with increasing speed, the value of intellectual property derives from the information or intellectual property it contains. These products are the main source of export revenue for most industrialized countries, but the United States, as the world leader in producing information-intensive technologies, holds the most valuable portfolio in high technology and, therefore, stands to lose the most to "pirates."

The strength of intellectual property protection in developing countries has a direct influence on the amount and type of technology transferred to them by advanced economies. The more information-intensive the technology—pharmaceuticals, chemicals, and electrical equipment—the greater the reluctance to transfer it in the absence of adequate intellectual property enforcement. For example, software, biotechnology, and semiconductor technologies all involve industries in which the value of the information contained in or stored by the technology exceeds by far the value of the physical or mechanical product containing the information.

A survey of developing countries developed by Buscaglia and Guerrero (1995) shows a direct association between the way a firm in the information-intensive sector (i.e., a sector where research and development represents more than 5 percent of total production costs) views intellectual property enforcement and the commitment of foreign direct investment. Some 49 percent of U.S. firms surveyed in the chemical and pharmaceutical industries stated that intellectual property protection in Argentina was too weak to permit transferring their best and latest technology to that country. For Colombia, the number was 55 percent; for Chile, 42 percent; for Mexico, 45 percent; and for Venezuela, 51 percent. Firms in other industries—transportation equipment, metals, and food—are not as reluctant to invest in developing countries as the information-intensive sectors. In surveys, no U.S. metals industry firm stated that intellectual property protection in Argentina, Brazil, Chile, Mexico, or Venezuela was too weak to permit its transferring its best and latest technology. In the food industry, the percentage of U.S. firms that felt intellectual property protection was too weak to permit transfer of their best and latest technology ranged from a high of 25 percent for Mexico to a low of 12 percent for Argentina, Chile, and Venezuela (Mansfield 1994).

Thus advanced economies find the strength of intellectual property protection abroad to be a fundamental factor in the decision to invest in a developing country. The United States lobbies more aggressively than any other country to raise standards of intellectual property protection in developing countries. Why? Because, as a leading scholar writes, "few other countries are willing to make a stink about piracy, even when they have lots to lose. . . . Potential allies, such as Japanese video-game makers, German and Swiss drug concerns and British and French filmmakers prefer to walk softly and let the United States carry the big stick" (Blount 1996, 12–15). The others let the United States put pressure on developing countries for them, but because 67 percent of U.S. exports are considered information intensive—compared to 44 percent for Germany and 51 percent for Japan—these other countries also have less to lose (Blount 1996).

With so much at stake, it is no wonder that advanced economies, led by the United States, have lobbied to raise the protection of intellectual property rights in developing countries to the level of the developed world. After all efforts have been made, however, the bottom line is that international treaties specifically devoted to intellectual property rights protection have been largely ineffective in dealing with piracy in developing countries.

TRADE-RELATED INTELLECTUAL PROPERTY RIGHTS: THE MULTILATERAL FRAMEWORK

As the case study above shows, legal reforms are the products of compromises brought on by domestic and foreign pressures. Today the United States, the European Union (EU), and Japan increasingly depend for their competitiveness on their ability to protect the value inherent in intellectual property. Most of the developing countries, in contrast, depend on low-tech exports to the advanced economies. Many of these exports benefit from the Generalized System of Preferences (GSP), which grants lower tariffs (or preferences) to designated exports from some developing countries. This interdependence encourages advanced and developing countries to resolve outstanding conflicts, particularly the problem of intellectual property rights. The developed countries' threat in these negotiations was of loss of access to the United States and European markets through the cancellation of GSP and the elimination of zero tariffs applied by advanced economies to selected products from benefiting countries. Foreign pressure, however, is not the only thing that brought legal reforms in developing countries; the WTO Treaty also assured access to the latest technologies they needed in a world where international competition, instead of import substitution, is the only road to development.

As stated above, for more than a century the enforcement mechanisms provided by the Paris and Berne conventions to protect international intellectual property rights were inadequate. They provided broad outlines but left important details to national legislation. But over time the provisions for dealing with enforcement became an increasing source of tensions for countries generating information-intensive goods and services. Since 1995, many developing countries under WTO supervision have adopted trade-related intellectual property rights (TRIPs) that are more compatible with U.S. and European minimum standards of protection. (Some commentators might even classify these legal reforms as "transplants.") As part of the GATT framework, the WTO agreement specifies that developing countries must (1) enforce a set of internationally recognized standards for incorporating the protection of intellectual property rights into national laws; (2) develop a consultation and dispute settlement mechanism for overseeing the implementation of the international norms; and (3) resolve any government-to-government disputes regarding the interpretation of such norms. This new agreement was a product of many diplomatic initiatives that, since the 1980s, have sought to alter the international intellectual property system and create a linkage with trade-related issues. The advanced economies also wanted to establish uniform standards of protection for intellectual property rights at a global level and improve enforcement mechanisms.

The preservation and observance of TRIPs—contained in the 1994 WTO agreement signed by all countries—are essential for sustaining the growth of international trade, investment, economic development, and, as some countries have noted, the beneficial distribution of technology. From an institutional standpoint, it is interesting to note that certain industrialized countries chose the

WTO as the mechanism to further legal harmonization in intellectual property rules because the WTO offers better guarantees for international dispute settlements in intellectual property issues. First, the WTO has a more fluid mechanism for adopting new measures; the members of WTO have not formed voting blocs, largely because of their varying economic interests in the many aspects of trade that are subject to the WTO negotiations. Second, WTO dispute settlement procedures, while viewed as needing considerable improvement, are generally considered better than those in the Paris and Berne conventions. Moreover, the WTO stipulates that authorized dispute settlement procedures enable treaty members to impose trade sanctions on countries infringing their intellectual property rights. Third, the WTO is the most appropriate forum today for the discussion of issues considered essential by developing countries. For example, GATT is a good place for working out compromises, such as lowering American and European agricultural subsidies (an important issue for many developing countries) and strengthening intellectual property protection (an important issue for developed countries). This led to the realization that "there would be no chance of liberalizing trade in services and providing better protection for intellectual property unless developing countries won genuine advantages in the Uruguay Round" (Buscaglia and Long 1997, 13–17).

To sum up, as a result of the foreign and domestic pressures discussed above, developing countries have been forced to reconsider many of their legal institutions, including their national intellectual property laws. Thus the international economic and political environment has worked to produce laws in developing countries aimed at protecting intellectual property. Thus we see how laws and regulations can evolve in a way that enhances business transactions and economic efficiency.

CHAPTER 2

Legal and Economic Integration: The Cases for and against Legal Transplants

Many reformers and the public generally tend to believe that legal reforms are rooted entirely in the traditions, customs, and values of individual nations. As we said in the preceding chapter, however, international legal transplants are one of the main sources of legal change in developing countries. The parochialism of many reformers and of the public clouds understanding of such change and leads people to disregard international legal doctrines, those "outside" laws that can help solve a social or economic problem. Mattei (1997) observes that many legal changes only appear to be derived from domestic roots. In most cases, and especially within the commercial domain, the norms of interaction transcend political frontiers; therefore, as the size of the market expands internationally, laws that address economic transactions in one country are transplanted to another country. In a sense, the adoption of a law is the product of a process in which many laws compete to be the prevailing one. For example, the legal rules governing trespass of private property in Germany, France, Italy, and the United States provide different solutions and different compensations. The economic impact of these alternative legal rules on efficiency can be assessed by applying statistics combined with the economic analysis of the law (i.e., jurimetrics).

Most developing countries have today chosen an export-led approach to economic growth and are thus eager to attract foreign direct investment (FDI). To enhance trade openness abroad, and at the same time attract foreign investment to their domestic markets, they must provide a stable environment in which to do business. Competitive pressures therefore force developing countries to harmonize their legal systems with those of countries exporting capital by incorporating foreign legal frameworks that firms in advanced economies think will enhance their security and productive efficiency.

In this context, a central topic must be the main economic factors explaining the process of legal transplants and legal integrations that tend to enhance productive efficiency. As stated in Ulen (1996, 9), "Law and Economics has been one of the most important and productive innovations in legal scholarship of the twentieth century. Yet its contributions to the issues of constitutional law, including federalism, are relatively modest." We could also add that the attention paid by the law and economics of development to the analysis of legal and economic integration has been insufficient.

The origin of law can be traced to several sources, ranging from the norms of behavior that govern interactions in a society to importing a legal doctrine from a different legal system—a legal transplant. The mechanisms through which parliaments and the judiciary in civil law countries isolate and translate norms into law require identifying standard practices in a society and the country's business communities. The efficiency of these practices must be ascertained with the aid of the theoretical and empirical tools of economists and other analysts. For example, using statistics in the analysis of the law can determine the impact of alternative doctrines on economic behavior. A legal doctrine, captured through an international transplant, could be economically assessed and compared to the economic impact of a doctrine that reflects the domestic norms of behavior in the society. Few empirical studies of this sort have been undertaken in law and economics or within the economic analysis of development. Yet studies by Long and Buscaglia (1997), Cooter and Ginsburg (1996), and Buscaglia and Guerrero (1995) have clearly shown the advantages of applying statistical techniques to the economic impact of the law in developing countries. Being able to assess empirically the economic impact of the law is key to public policymaking and represents a clear improvement in the analysis of the economic impact of differing legal reforms considered for adoption in developing countries.

Many may argue that civil law systems would tend to reject an economic analysis of their laws. Yet, quoting Cooter (1996, 145), "Judges allegedly make law in civil systems by interpreting codes, not finding social norms. Compared to common law countries, the codifiers in civil systems apparently have more influence and the judges allegedly have less influence. Interpreting some codes, however, looks a lot like finding social norms. Comparative lawyers, consequently, debate whether the apparent differences in the two systems are real or illusory." From this perspective, we say, civil law systems generally have the capacity to react to efficiency even if not as openly as common law systems. In fact the civil law originally evolved as a common law system. In Watson (1978) we find an excellent account of this evolution. Before the nineteenth century, the European *ius commune,* or common law, was based on the judge's interpretation of Roman law in the context of local norms and practices. Starting with the French Revolution, the centralization of lawmaking through legislatures aimed at replacing laws based on social norms with rules that were designed and rationally engineered to bring a better way of life to society. Under this new system, the judge was not supposed to find norms but only to interpret and apply laws generated by legislatures. Although this post–French Revolution framework took power away from the judicial branch and made it more dependent on the legislative power of parliament, this new interpretation and application of laws was also subject to an implicit and subtle application of social norms as inputs in the opinions of judges. Thus, in the civil law system, judges and parliaments possess a joint capacity to make laws—parliament in a formal and open way and judges in a more hidden fashion—regaining some of the power they had exercised before the revolution, especially when they address legal gaps or interpret vague statutes enacted by parliament.

LEGAL INTEGRATION AND
ECONOMIC DEVELOPMENT

Legal integration is the adoption by two or more legal systems of the same set of rules for interaction within a well-specified social domain. Therefore, legal integration is another source of legal change that can affect efficiency in many developing countries. Of central interest is why governments choose one strategy over another in pursuing legal/economic integration. Buscaglia and Long (1997) propose that a successful legal/economic integration is a function of the convergence of three broad conditions: (1) the compatibility of political systems; (2) the public sector's expectation of gains from liberalizing international trade; and (3) the private sector's expectation of gains from regionalizing production, transferring capital and technology, and harmonizing trade-related rules. Some or all of these factors are key driving forces behind the main trade agreements within the Western Hemisphere, Europe, and Asia: the North American Free Trade Agreement (NAFTA) of the United States, Canada, and Mexico; the Andean Pact, consisting of Bolivia, Colombia, Ecuador, Peru, and Venezuela; the Common Market of the South (Mercosur), which includes Argentina, Brazil, Chile, Paraguay, and Uruguay; the European Union; and the Asian economic bloc. The empirical verification of these three broad conditions can be found in the case study of Mercosur later in this chapter.

Economic transformations in many developing countries have created a need for major new legal developments. What are the main economic forces pushing the drive to integrate economic and legal systems? A statistical and legal analysis of Latin America by Buscaglia and Long (1997) shows that the growth in trade between the same economic sectors of two countries (i.e., international intrasectoral trade) goes hand in hand with the private sector's growing demand for the harmonization of trade-related laws. Harmonization of laws occurs in many areas: banking, insurance, securities, liberal professions, international securities exchange regulations, and transportation. In other words, harmonization of the rules occurs principally within commercial law. Therefore, we see that the future of integration and trade processes necessarily entails the deepening and development of these legal areas.

Economic history, however, is littered with the hulls of ship-wrecked trade agreements seeking legal integration (Kindleberger 1996). That is why the compatibility of two or more legal systems must be a factor in the legal integration of countries. Moreover, an empirical analysis of patterns of trade in Buscaglia and Long (1997) shows that legal compatibility is driven by similarities in economic structures.

LEGAL AND ECONOMIC INTEGRATION

During the 1980s, increasing competition and volatility in world markets induced industrialized and developing countries to cluster together in regional economic blocs. This trend was spurred by three factors: (1) technological innovations in transportation and commu-nications that expanded the markets for an increasing number of goods and services; (2) the overall economic slowdown in world trade during the 1988–92 period, accelerated by the collapse of the communist regimes; and (3) the near failure of the multilateral trade negotiations sponsored by GATT at the Uruguay Round. In turn, the near-breakdown in multilateral trade negotiations served to create an environment compatible with bilateral and regional accords.

Recent studies of regional legal and economic integration have stressed the key role of emerging trade blocs in shaping the world economy of the twenty-first century (Davey, Jackson, and Sykes 1995). Economic trends—such as rapid changes in applied research, technology, capital flows, and trade patterns—have all assumed an enhanced importance in fostering economic growth. According to Abramowitz (1989), the extent to which a country that is techno-logically behind is able to catch up depends in part on its capability to absorb advanced technologies. Porter (1985) states that the main factors fostering the social capability for technological improvement include a strong research and development (R&D) sector, institu-tions of higher education satisfying the demand for scientists and engineers, and competitive environments acting as disciplinary factors for firms. None of the aforementioned works, however, dis-cusses in depth the legal changes needed to foster competitive envi-ronments and enhance capabilities to absorb technologies.

Developing nations currently face a unique growth opportunity created by global free trade, the continuous decline in transportation and communication costs, the unprecedented availability of generic applied knowledge, and the expanding flows of international financial investments. Many of these countries, however, lack the institutional capability to create or absorb applied knowledge. Legal and economic reforms are based on strategies that give the private sector a more important role in economic development and in some cases strengthen the foundations for economic growth. In part these reforms consist in liberalizing trade and integrating markets.

Experiments in regional integration differ appreciably. For instance, the Andean Pact in Latin America denotes a free trade area in which the main goal is the eventual elimination of trade restrictions, whereas the Asean in Southeast Asia provides only for trade and economic cooperation on a limited and loose basis. In contrast, the Mercosur trade agreement in South America and the European Union encompass free trade areas plus more ambitious goals related to institutional harmonization of substantive bodies of laws and regulations. The Mercosur trade agreement, enacted in March 1991, is the most ambitious attempt yet toward regional integration, including fostering legal harmonization. Moreover, four working groups involving all countries in Latin America except Cuba—the Andean Pact, Mercosur, NAFTA, and Caricom (Caribbean Community)—have started negotiating the harmonization of laws in areas including health, the deterrence of organized crime, environmental protection, rules of foreign investment, dispute settlement, sanitation, smaller economies and subsidies, antidumping and countervailing duties, government procurement, intellectual property rights, services, and competition policy.

LEGAL AND ECONOMIC INTEGRATION: THE CASE OF LATIN AMERICA

This section briefly describes the main drives toward legal integration in South America during the nineteenth and twentieth centuries, including a legal-statistical analysis demonstrating the connections between legal integration and economic structures.

Most of the civil law countries in Latin America achieved their independence in the nineteenth century and, one after the other, adopted codified continental-style European law. Much of the codification observed in Latin American legal history until the early twentieth century was the result of transplanting civil, commercial, and penal codes from Europe to the different countries in the region (Watson 1983). Between 1825 and 1890, substantive and procedural civil, commercial, and criminal codes were all transplanted from the French codification with few adaptations to the South American scene (Merryman 1985). For example, Argentina, Bolivia, Brazil, Chile, Colombia, Ecuador, Peru, and Venezuela adopted the Napoleonic Code, even though they had never been under French territorial control. The impact of the American Constitution on Latin American public law—in form if not in substance—is another example of a transplant. Therefore, we can say that most Latin American legal systems started from the same evolutionary bases as transplants from Europe and the United States.

Legal systems become more complex as they evolve. This complexity is seen in the breadth of social-economic interactions the legal system is capable of addressing. As an economy evolves from its agrarian origins to a more industrialized stage, the legal system that supports the economic interactions of the developing society tends to branch out from its original base as well. This is done to reduce the costs of interaction in new types of transactions within the more advanced economic structure. In fact, this explains why legal systems in still largely agrarian countries including Bolivia, Somalia, Kenya, and Peru have not changed much over time when compared to the legal systems of the more dynamic countries including Argentina, Chile, and South Korea.

Examples of linked economic and legal change can be found in the evolution of commercial law in Latin America. Manufacturing and service sectors began to emerge while the gold standard ruled international trade, which inspired a widespread Latin American integration of its economic and legal institutions (Merryman 1985). There is a rich historical background (over a century and a half) of Latin American countries addressing legal harmonization driven by international trade and economic change. Recall that legal harmonization tends to occur among countries with similarities in their economic structures; legal transplants are usually the attempt of one country to adopt the legal doctrines of another country with a higher level of economic development (Buscaglia and Long 1997).

The First Treaty of Lima, signed in 1848 by Argentina, Brazil, Chile, Colombia, and Peru, contains rules according to which contracts signed and documents executed in one signatory republic were valid and enforced by judges and courts in the other countries as well. At the Congress of Lima in 1864–65, Argentina, Brazil, Chile, and Peru adopted postal, trade, and navigation treaties committing them to providing all possible facilities and protection to trade "as one of the most effective means of promoting the development and growth of industry and wealth and making a future Confederation of states more secure and prosperous" (Velez Muniz 1951; Acevedo 1987). Further, the trade and navigation treaties of 1864 provide that all natives or nationals of contracting Latin American states are considered equals with regard to a wide range of matters. This was the legal foundation of the later Latin American principle of equality of nationals and foreigners with respect to international liability of states in cases of torts and/or property damage. Argentina, Brazil, and Chile launched initiatives that led to the Congress of Jurists (1877–80) in Lima and a treaty establishing uniform rules of private international law (Acevedo 1987).

The Second Congress of Jurists, held in 1888–89 in Montevideo, produced eight treaties and an additional protocol sponsored and drafted by Argentine, Brazilian, and Chilean jurists. The treaties covered procedural law, literary and artistic property, patents for inventions, trademarks and brand names, international criminal law, and international civil law. The protocol contained general rules for applying the laws of any of the contracting states in the territories of the others. Finally, South American countries for which international trade was a significantly increasing portion of national economic activity (Argentina, Brazil, Chile, and Peru) proposed a major step in legal integration. Their intention to codify international law was recognized in the Convention for the Formation of Codes on Public and Private International Law, signed in 1902, and in the Convention on International Law, signed at the Inter-American Conference of Rio de Janeiro in 1906. Both treaties established methods and procedures to further the process of legal codification and cooperation at the inter-American level. In all these cases, the countries pushing for legal harmonization were experiencing changes in their trade-related economic structures associated with domestic legal changes (Buscaglia 1996).

Thus, since the closing decades of the nineteenth century, Latin American states have been trying to codify private international law. This work has taken different institutional forms over time. The main approaches stretched from global—contemplating a single body of rules covering all aspects of private law—to a more gradual and progressive process that involved drafting specific international instruments (Buscaglia 1996; Acevedo 1987). The approach of drafting a single code prevailed during the aforementioned 1877 Congress of Lima and culminated in the adoption of a single code of international law, the Bustamante Code, at the Sixth International Conference of American States in Havana in 1928. Beginning in the 1960s, within the framework of the Organization of American States (OAS), the Inter-American Juridical Committee tried to codify all the different areas of private international law. The committee proposed to review the Bustamante Code to determine whether it was possible to merge its provisions with those of the Montevideo treaties of 1889 and 1939–40. It drafted a code that was not, however, supported by all the member states of the OAS. Those countries supporting legal integration were in all cases the countries with the most dynamic economic sectors (Argentina, Brazil, and Chile); reservations and opposition emerged among those who still had the more traditional agricultural economies (Bolivia, Colombia, Paraguay, Peru, Venezuela) (Acevedo 1987).

Having failed in its global objective because of the different levels of economic development in the more advanced and the less advanced countries, the OAS turned to sectoral codification by scheduling intergovernmental meetings to deal with special technical matters and to develop special aspects of inter-American cooperation. The effort continues today through the Specialized Conferences on Private International Law (CIDIP) under the auspices of the

TABLE 2

LEGAL CHANGES VERSUS ECONOMIC STRUCTURE
DURING 1850–1995

Country	Number of Amendments in Commercial Codes	Number of Trade-Related Nonagricultural Sectors	Number of Interest Agreements
Argentina	739	37	96
Bolivia	4	3	13
Brazil	771	41	116
Chile	593	27	60
Colombia	9	5	36
Ecuador	19	13	30
Peru	10	5	23
Uruguay	11	6	4
Venezuela	71	22	20

United Nations. To date, five CIDIP have been held: Panama in 1975, Montevideo in 1979, La Paz in 1984, Montevideo in 1989, and Mexico in 1994.

Buscaglia and Long (1997) have shown that Argentina, Brazil, and Chile started to address new types of economic interactions legally as a result of their higher levels of specialization and division of labor within domestic markets. As the relative growth of their agricultural sectors diminished and manufacturing increased, commercial codes became subject to major redrafting. Table 2 contrasts the dynamic economies of Argentina, Brazil, and Chile to the more traditional economies of Bolivia, Colombia, Ecuador, and Venezuela during the 1850–1995 period. More specifically, the table shows the number of amendments introduced to commercial codes, the number of nonagricultural trade-related manufacturing and service sectors where growth in sales exceeded 5 percent annually, and the number of international legal agreements within the commercial area for each country.

A strong correlation exists between the emergence of high-growth nonagricultural "new" sectors (i.e., more and stronger industrial and service sectors) and legal change. For example, during the 1890–1995 period, Argentina, Brazil, and Chile had the most dynamic economies in the sectors of agro-manufacturing, minerals, steel, financial services, transportation, and energy. They also had the largest number of amendments to their commercial laws and signed the largest number of trade-related legal treaties. At the same time, these dynamic economies were more likely to harmonize their legal systems through international legal agreements in areas related to tangible and intangible property, contractual rules, family, torts, competition, and government procurement. Thus, as an increasing number of business exchanges occur in countries with overlapping, growing trade-related sectors, the need for legal harmonization tends to increase.

TRADE AND LEGAL CONVERGENCE

As explained above, domestic and international forces press for a high degree of convergence in the legal systems of developing countries within the commercial areas subject to international trade. One example is the international legal convergence since 1985, based on transplants in intellectual property laws. These reflect the developing countries' recognition that an increasing proportion of their imports in the form of information-intensive goods and services originate in the industrialized countries (Buscaglia and Guerrero 1995). The Paris and Berne conventions governed the international protection of intellectual property for more than a century, but the weak enforcement capacity of their administering organ—the World Intellectual Property Organization (WIPO)—created the need for a new and more effective legal framework. While the WIPO dithered, those countries generating the most information-intensive products began to apply unilateral pressures on developing countries from Egypt to Argentina. Advanced-country firms generating these technologies started to demand the use of trade sanctions, threats of withdrawal of trade benefits, as a way to punish less-developed countries' unauthorized use of intellectual property (Pearl 1996; Restivo 1997).

Developing countries, by contrast, manifested their adherence to two fundamental principles to justify their legal environments: First, the principle of *territoriality*, based on the premise that property rights needed to be honored according to each state's domestic rules. In Latin America, this principle is applied in the international intellectual property arena through the *Calvo Doctrine,* which maintains that "aliens are only entitled to those legal rights and privileges enjoyed by nationals, and hence may seek redress for grievances only before local authorities and to the extent permitted by local law" (Alden 1976, 136). The second principle, known as *independence,* indicated that the definition of rights within one state does not force other states to grant the same rights. Clearly, these two principles are incompatible with the international harmonization of laws and economic integration promoted today by developed countries. Therefore, led by the United States, countries generating technologies started to rely heavily on the application of unilateral pressure to stop the infringement of their intellectual property rights. Suspension of preferential tariffs and trade sanctions were the most common policy tools for punishing developing countries. As an example, Section 301 of the 1988 U.S. Trade Act authorizes the U.S. government to reduce or eliminate generalized system of preferences (GSP) benefits (i.e., preferential tariffs) and to impose import restrictions or even retaliatory measures. These legal tools were a very serious matter to many developing countries, given the importance to them of the North American and European markets. The North American market absorbed 41.1 percent of overall exports from Latin America and 62 percent of all exports from Africa between 1983 and 1988, with no fewer than eight countries of the region placing more than half their exports there. Mexico, for instance, sends almost 55 percent of its exports by volume to the U.S. market; Colombia, Peru, and Venezuela send between 30 and 40 percent; Brazil about 30 percent; and Argentina approximately 18 percent of total exports (see World Bank 1996, Statistical Abstract). These kinds of foreign pressures explain the legal convergence observed in areas covering trade-related competition rules, financial markets, and government procurement.

Developing countries' early attempts at integration were conceived as an integral part of the import-substituting industrialization (ISI) explained above. This inward-looking strategy was conceived and understood as a "collective defense" for sheltering poor countries from adverse fluctuations in the world economy. Many developing countries have markets too small to achieve effective economies of scale. The strategy of import substitution, strongly supported for several decades by the Economic Commission for Latin America (ECLA), a branch of the United Nations known in Latin America by its Spanish name, *Comisión Económica para América Latina* (or CEPAL), seemed to have a solution. For ECLA/CEPAL, regional integration offered a way to provide markets large enough to satisfy economies of scale that in turn would presumably strengthen the import-substitution process. Nonreciprocity and preferential treatment were to be granted in accordance with, or dependent on, the level of economic development of individual countries. Tariff barriers against countries outside the region would serve to protect developing countries' products and enable them to compete more effectively against foreign imports. This form of trade seemed to offer the possibility of overcoming the problem of small size and market by providing larger regional markets that would mean a greater volume of trade and better opportunities to specialize.

At any time, geographic proximity facilitates trade flows across borders, but today regional integration has assumed a new meaning. In the 1950s and 1960s the prescription for regional integration was defensive and tended to promote an inward-looking economic model. The emphasis today is on an offensive export-led growth, where regional integration is understood as an element of the overall outward-oriented strategy. The new strategy forced many countries, including Argentina, Brazil, and Uganda, to reconsider many of their institutions and begin to adopt legal frameworks that are converging toward the bodies of laws prevailing in countries exporting information-intensive goods and services. When trade-driven institutional harmonization became the new development strategy throughout the developing world (Buscaglia 1993), international trade-related legal frameworks constituted the first wave of legal changes in poor countries. Laws covering trade under GATT's Uruguay Round (now WTO)—intellectual property, foreign investment regulations, competition rules, government procurement, and trade sanctions related to business transactions—were all later subject to domestic legal revisions or enactments in developing countries.

The new international economic and political environments described above have started to force low-income countries' legal standards to converge toward the legal frameworks of the nations generating standard technologies. For example, with the privatization of state monopolies in the developing world and the shift toward import competition there came a vast increase in the demand for high-technology products. The great increase in international transactions in information-intensive goods and services (e.g., biotech products) made it necessary to reformulate the legal foundation of intellectual property to (1) define and enforce the rights of those businesses generating high technology and (2) facilitate the diffusion of know-how to those countries with the capacity to absorb it. It soon became clear that the international harmonization of intellectual property rules was a sine qua non for the smooth transfer of complex technologies to the developing world.

Many low- and medium-income countries' experiments aimed at legal harmonization, however, have failed to produce substantive results or at least anywhere near the results developed countries sought (Buscaglia and Long 1997). This failure was due to many factors, ranging from the broad cultural impediments noted earlier to a lack of private sector lobbying for compatible legal solutions on trade issues. Addressing the latter, countries with similar economic structures (i.e., where the relative weight of economic sectors is similar) that trade with each other (such as the Canadian and American automobile industries) have private sectors that demand compatible legal frameworks within their product areas. The fact that parallel economic sectors (e.g., the chemical industry) sponsor similar legal rules may explain the drive toward the harmonization of intellectual property and competition regulations from Argentina, Brazil, and Chile in Latin America to Hong Kong, Taiwan, and Singapore in Asia.

Imagine two types of countries hoping to harmonize their commercial laws. On the one hand are countries such as Bolivia and Uruguay, where private commercial laws have developed little over time and where there are no industrial or service sectors producing information-intensive products. On the other hand are countries like Argentina, Brazil, and Chile, which have relatively complex commercial legal systems and a much higher proportion of their trade concentrated on industrial and service-related sectors. The data in table 2 suggest that legal harmonization would be more difficult between the two groups of countries than among countries in one or the other group. In the former category, the private sectors within each group demand different kinds of commercial legal frameworks, making legal integration through either harmonization or transplants more difficult to achieve.

Consider private sector firms in Bolivia that are importing Brazilian computer software and hardware, compact discs, or movies. The Bolivians do not have an incentive to lobby at home for the enactment of intellectual property, government procurement, or competition laws compatible with the needs and interests of the Brazilian firms. Buscaglia and Long (1997) show that the main drive to harmonize trade-related laws was among countries with high levels of international trade between the same industrial and service-related sectors (i.e., intrasectoral trade). For example, Brazil and Argentina, with the highest levels of intrasectoral trade in Latin America, are also the countries with the highest levels of international trade-related legal agreements, as shown by the number of legal agreements reached between 1890 and 1990 in table 2. That is, the industries with the highest levels of intrasectoral trade within the region—among them automotive, energy, steel, pharmaceuticals, minerals, and textiles—were also the main forces lobbying for legal harmonization of standards and regulations.

Thus the practice has been for the relatively larger developing countries, with their larger trade flows, to seek harmonious relations with their main trading partners through legal agreements. The success of these efforts has varied considerably even among major trading countries, however, as is evident when one examines the case of the largest trader of them all, China, where cultural and other often overlooked factors are paramount (Alford 1995; Potter 1995; Epstein 1994). The smaller developing countries more often look for a "free ride" by transplanting bodies of the law to their own environment. With these experiences in mind, we can better understand the history of failures in legal harmonization. For example, in 1961 the Kennedy administration and Latin American countries launched the ambitious Latin American Free Trade Association (LAFTA). But despite good intentions—it was in the midst of import-substitution industrialization (ISI) regional policies—its member states failed to agree on what the economic and legal integration process should encompass. This led to the demise of LAFTA before the end of the decade (Acevedo 1987). All the main opponents of this treaty were countries with more than 90 percent of their exports in primary products and little or no interest or background in legal integration.

CASE STUDY: MERCOSUR AND LEGAL INTEGRATION

Economic integration and growth among developing countries have created a need for major new legal reforms. Today the private sector is the driving force behind legal initiatives related to the Free Trade Agreement for the Americas (FTA) and the European Union (EU). The FTA, for example, aims at forming a customs union covering the entire Western Hemisphere by the year 2005. Meetings of trade ministers from thirty-four countries have received practical recommendations from private sector leaders on subjects ranging from harmonization of investment regulations to environmental laws. The FTA has bogged down, as has the anticipated admission of Chile to NAFTA, mainly because the U.S. government—the executive and legislature—has failed to follow up on its commitments for domestic political reasons.

Under these circumstances, the Mercosur (Mercado Comun del Sur; Common Market of the South) Trade Agreement, signed by Argentina, Brazil, Paraguay, and Uruguay, constitutes what might be termed the *great leap forward* approach to economic and institutional integration. Because Mercosur is dynamic and the FTA is anemic, many other countries in Latin America have applied for associate membership—that is, membership without the common external tariff—in Mercosur. Mercosur's dynamism is a result of intelligent Argentinean and Brazilian leaders taking advantage of this international situation. Contrary to conventional theory, which views economic integration as a gradual process achieved through a series of stages, the Mercosur countries have chosen to bypass several intermediate steps, with the avowed aim of quickly having a common market in place. This common market would consist of (1) a free trade zone with zero trade tariffs and nontariff barriers, (2) a common external tariff, and (3) integrated trade-related institutions (e.g., a conflict resolution forum).

As stated above, the import substitution policies followed in most developing countries during the 1960s and 1970s isolated their industrialized sectors from international trade, and private sectors did not bother to push for legal predictability outside their local markets. Nor was legal/economic integration then on the private sectors' agenda. The demise of the import substitution model, however, created an environment in which all development-oriented parties looked favorably on trade and legal harmonization. In 1986 in South America's southern cone Argentina and Brazil decided to put aside their long-standing rivalry to enter into a cooperative relationship termed the Argentine-Brazilian Economic Integration Program (ABEIP), a formal program for economic, legal, and political cooperation. The political objective of the ABEIP was to strengthen the infant democratic regimes that had emerged after prolonged periods of military rule in each country. More obviously, the economic goal of the ABEIP was to expand and diversify bilateral trade between these two countries via protocols that emphasized, on a sector-by-sector basis, such domestic products as capital goods, agribusiness, and the automotive sector (Baldinelli 1990). In August 1989 Presidents Raúl Alfonsín of Argentina and José Sarney of Brazil signed an integration treaty, which was ratified by the two congresses, announcing their intention to create a free trade area over a ten-year period. In reality, the relatively favorable economic situation that had prompted Argentina and Brazil to embark on the ABEIP in 1986 turned sour because of (1) a chaotic macroeconomic environment in both countries (i.e., hyperinflation and recession) and (2) external constraints imposed by the two countries' foreign debts. Thus, despite a few advances, most of the protocols were never executed. But by the end of the decade, Argentina and Brazil were in deep economic crises, and the failure to coordinate their economic policies, in addition to the cumbersome protocols, complicated bilateral negotiations and brought all progress toward economic integration to an end (Chudnovsky 1992).

Misgivings about the future of the projected integration were quickly dispelled, however, when new presidents took office in the two countries: Carlos Menem in Argentina in mid-1989 and Fernando Collor de Mello in Brazil in early 1990. Both presidents dropped import substitution and adopted realistic and potentially productive policies. They tried to deal with their stagnant economies, lack of resources, and foreign debts by adopting free-market economic policies that differed appreciably from those of their predecessors. Indeed, economic and legal integration was a key component of both their foreign policies. In July 1990, Menem and Collor de Mello signed the Buenos Aires Act, which called for establishing a common market by the end of 1994 and institutional integration by the year 2000. This act introduced a new phase, broadening the scope of the proposed integration and shortening its timetable. Equally important was the fact that both countries pursued integration within the context of programs for unilateral trade liberalization and legal harmonization related to government procurement, foreign investment rules, intellectual property, and competition.

In August 1990, only a month later, Paraguay and Uruguay joined the proposed integration scheme. On 26 March 1991 the foreign ministers of the four countries signed the Treaty of Asunción, which called for the creation of Mercosur. The four parties agreed that Argentina and Brazil would comply with all provisos of the treaty by 31 December 1994, while the deadline for Paraguay and Uruguay to do so would be 31 December 1995. By that time, it was felt, Mercosur would constitute a common market. The main provisions of the Treaty of Asunción were

1.   An across-the-board tariff reduction.

2.   The coordination of macroeconomic policies.

3.   The establishment of a common external tariff.

4.   The development of accords for specific sectors of the economy to optimize the use and mobility of labor and capital while achieving economies of scale.

5. The implementation of an institutional framework to resolve trade litigation.

6. The creation of the Council of the Common Market, Mercosur's highest decision-making institution, made up of the ministers of finance, justice, and foreign affairs of each country. The council would be entrusted with the authority to establish general policy guidelines between 1991 and 2005 in accordance with the provisions of the treaty.

7. The creation of the Common Market Group (CMG), the executive arm of Mercosur. The CMG, consisting of four permanent and four alternate representatives from the ministries of foreign affairs, finance, justice, and central bank of each country, was to assist the Council of the Common Market by taking care of technical aspects of the negotiation process. The CMG's activities would be coordinated by the ministers of foreign affairs of the four countries. The group would act on the recommendations of ten subgroups (trade, customs, commercial law, monetary and fiscal matters related to trade, land transport, maritime transport, industrial and technological issues, agriculture, energy, and macroeconomic coordination), dealing with policy issues sector by sector.

From the beginning there was considerable skepticism regarding the possibility of establishing a common market of such ambitious goals in so short a time. Yet the very ambitiousness of the project was intended to demonstrate the seriousness with which the four presidents approached the task of regional integration. The deadlines were chosen to coincide with the end of the presidential terms of the four founding presidents. Thus the outgoing presidents hoped to lock their successors into the integration process.

In an effort to pave the way for integration, three later summits followed at six-month intervals. The first, in the Argentine resort of Las Leñas in June 1992, instituted (1) a timetable for coordinating the establishment of Mercosur by 1 January 1995, (2) a timetable for harmonizing macroeconomic policies so as to meet the above deadline, (3) harmonization of laws to ensure that binational Argentine-Brazilian enterprises would receive treatment equivalent to that accorded national enterprises, and (4) procedures for handling complaints related to unfair trade competition.

The second summit, held on 28 December 1992 in Montevideo, Uruguay, found the Mercosur partners at odds with one another over domestic policies that tended to jeopardize certain basic tenets of the Asunción Treaty. For example, Argentina had raised its "statistical" levy from 3 percent to 10 percent as a way of protecting its domestic industry from competition with cheap Brazilian imports. Problems were compounded by developments in Brazil: (1) a deepening economic recession and (2) the accession of Itamar Franco as president, replacing the recently ousted Collor de Mello, which raised uncertainties about Mercosur's future. Nevertheless, all the presidents reaffirmed their commitment to establishing a common market and removing all trade barriers within Mercosur by December 1995. They also agreed to discuss a proposal, put forth by one of the subgroups, to establish a common external tariff that would range from 0 to 20 percent.

The third summit, held on 1 July 1993 in Asunción, Paraguay, adopted a common external tariff (CET) as originally planned. In addition, it set the list of laws to be harmonized. The list included the definition of the regulatory tools needed to implement a dispute resolution mechanism within Mercosur, foreign investment regulations, and government procurement rules.

Peter Smith (1993, 2) notes one of the critical factors in economic and legal integration: "Political considerations play crucial roles in regional integration schemes. The most successful integration experiences have political purposes that are central to the overall mission." In fact, some scholars feel that one reason regional integration schemes in Latin America have had such a poor track record in the past has been their lack of a clearly defined political agenda directing the economic objectives (Mols 1993). Mercosur has placed consolidating democracy and preserving peace in the Southern Cone among its paramount political objectives. After Great Britain defeated Argentina in the 1982 Falklands/Malvinas war, the militaries from Argentina and Brazil withdrew from power, and security concerns based on military considerations fell to an all-time low. For the civilian administrations that ensued, security took on a new meaning: the preservation of regional peace and democracy. As Alberto van Klaveren (1993, 119) has pointed out:

> Transitions to democracy coincide with and are, at least in part, responsible for the quest for integration. [Mercosur] . . . is based on the assumption that membership is restricted to democratic governments and that integration can be seen as a guarantee against coups d'etat.

This position was acted on in 1997 when the Mercosur countries and the United States intervened in the attempted coup in Paraguay.

The decision of Presidents Menem and Collor de Mello to broaden the original Alfonsín-Sarney agreements has been a remarkable political accomplishment, bringing stability to the region. Since this agreement, Argentina and Brazil have been able to cooperate on many issues, including transport and communications, nuclear proliferation (Argentina and Brazil signed a nuclear nonproliferation treaty in 1991), environmental protection, military cooperation, illegal immigration, and drug-related money laundering. Thus, in recent years security has taken on a broad political and economic meaning, incorporating the promotion of democracy, the enhancement of domestic competitiveness within the world economy, the penetration of new markets, and the improvement of member countries' bargaining position in international trade negotiations. Indeed, Mercosur allows the member countries to increase their bargaining in dealings with other trading blocks of the industrialized world to a much greater extent than would be possible if each country had tried the go-it-alone strategy.

Through Mercosur, South American leaders developed a common agenda of policy priorities, which was then negotiated in the General Agreement on Tariffs and Trade (GATT), as well as with the members of the NAFTA and the European Union (Hirst 1992). In this context, Mercosur took two important steps: (1) in 1992 it asked the WTO (GATT) to grant it recognition as a regional organization and (2) it signed an interinstitutional agreement with the

EU involving institutional support, technical assistance, and personnel training. Mercosur also opened discussions with the United States in 1993 to explore the possibility of forging an agreement between Mercosur and NAFTA.

Meanwhile, the private sectors of Argentina and Brazil affirmed their commitment to pushing forward with legal and economic integration. An economic/legal agenda seems to have been the guiding principle behind the Argentine-Brazilian scheme (ABEIP) and, later, that of Mercosur as well. In the first three years of its existence, Mercosur spurred a booming trade among its partners, racking up substantial annual increases: $5.1 billion in 1991; $7.5 billion in 1992; $8 billion by 1993 (Mols 1993), and rising to $9.5 billion in 1997 (National Council 1998). Despite the 1998–99 slowdown in trade caused by the Asian-related recession affecting Argentina and Brazil, experts expect intra-Mercosur trade to continue growing (*Statistical Abstract*, Foundation of Latin American Economic Research [FIEL], 1998). In terms of total exports, Argentine sales to Brazil jumped from 4.3 percent in 1983 to 19 percent in 1993 (Mols 1993, 11–12), and in 1997 those sales kept growing at an average rate equal to 14 percent (Ministerio de Economia, Argentina, *1998 Report*). Thus Mercosur has provided its members with overlapping business interests with incentives and the means to diversify and expand their exports.

Buscaglia and Long (1997) showed that countries that exchange a large proportion of exports and imports with one another within the same economic sectors—intrasectoral trade (e.g., exports and imports between the car industries in Brazil and Argentina)—will tend to promote an international harmonization of legal rules to their economic sectors. On the basis of the analytic framework introduced by Buscaglia and Long, we expect that the large proportion of international trade based on intrasectoral exchanges between Argentina and Brazil—and maybe Chile if it becomes a full member of Mercosur—will cause the private sectors in those countries to demand harmony in the rules of international trade. This simply means that a bottom-up (i.e., business-promoted) legal framework will emerge when there is enough overlapping in economic structures trading across borders to demand compatible legal rules that will permit a reduction in transaction costs.

In the vanguard will be the likes of the chemical and automotive sectors, with the agro-manufacturing, computer-related, food manufacturing, energy, and textiles industries joining in (Hirst 1993). These sectors have already actively supported Mercosur-related policies through lobbying in the Argentine and Brazilian legislatures. These sectors also supported GATT and its copyright and trademark laws (both important sources of rents for information-intensive exports) and the establishment of reliable dispute resolution mechanisms such as those proposed in the Treaty of Asunción. In contrast, the private sectors in Uruguay and Paraguay, both relatively agrarian economies, did not have the same incentives to support the harmonization of laws enhancing manufacturing activities. This is shown by the large number of Mercosur-originated agreements that have not been ratified by the Uruguayan or Paraguayan legislatures in contrast to the large number of those same agreements that have been enacted in Argentina and Brazil (Buscaglia 1997). By the late 1990s the process of generating Mercosur-related international agreements had become subject to ups and downs of the economic cycles of the main players in this trading bloc, Argentina and Brazil. Yet, economic cycles notwithstanding, Argentine and Brazilian private firms have taken the lead in this integration effort.

Mercosur has also provided the legal framework for sector-by-sector agreements among private entrepreneurial associations that have contributed to the harmonization of the aforementioned rules. For example, Argentine and Brazilian associations of steel producers signed an accord regulating bilateral trade, patents, competition, and government procurement rules; similar agreements are being negotiated in other business sectors.

In short, within Mercosur Argentina and Brazil have overlapping economic structures that support legal harmonization, whereas Uruguay and Paraguay are simply playing along to expand the markets for their primary exports. On the basis of historical experience and the lack of compatible interests, Paraguay's and Uruguay's private sectors have not shown interest in promoting the entire Mercosur agenda, making the future of Mercosur uncertain.

LEGAL HARMONIZATIONS VERSUS LEGAL TRANSPLANTS: LESSONS FOR THE FUTURE

This chapter explains why developing countries—some more than others—tend to harmonize and integrate their legal frameworks, as illustrated by the Mercosur case study. We show that outside pressures on developing countries in the context of the changing world economy, in addition to domestic crises within the developing world, have combined to create the environmental requirements and incentives needed for the emergence of legal integration and legal transplants. We have analyzed this legal and economic integration, noting that legal integration can be partially explained by the degree of overlap found in the economic structures of the countries involved in trade agreements. More specifically, the larger the bilateral intrasectoral trade in a country is, the more the private sector will demand the harmonization of national trade-related laws. Finally, the propensity of a country to seek international legal commercial agreements depends on the degree to which that country's economic system is compatible with other countries' economic systems. This being the case, traditional agrarian economies exclude themselves from seeking international legal harmonization/integration. As a result, agrarian economies have two choices when facing efficiency-enhancing legal reform: to transplant selected laws from abroad or to simply codify into law their preexisting domestic uses and customs.

CHAPTER 3

Procedural Aspects of the Law and Economic Development

THE JUDICIARY AND ECONOMIC DEVELOPMENT

As developing countries proceed with market reforms, the need for well-functioning dispute resolution mechanisms and procedures becomes increasingly evident. Yet the economic analysis of legal procedures and their impact on development are in their infancy. As stated in Buscaglia and Domingo (1997), the increasing complexity of social interactions due to democratization, growing urbanization, and the adoption of market reforms has created additional demands and thus need for dispute resolution services throughout the region. In addition, the shift of most economic transactions toward the market domain and away from the public administrative sphere of the state has created an unprecedented increase in private sector demands for an improved definition of rights and obligations.

In this context, it is becoming increasingly clear that the judiciary is as important for sound economic development as infrastructure and factories. The judicial system, which includes all the mechanisms needed to interpret and apply laws and regulations, is the main link through which the economic impact of the legal system is felt. Specifically, the three most important productive activities of the judicial sector within the economic system are (1) resolving conflicts, (2) upholding the principle of legality, and (3) penalizing legal infringements. All these roles are key to increasing fairness and predictability and thus reducing uncertainty in social interaction and diminishing transaction costs in the marketplace.

Judiciaries in most developing countries, however, suffer from increasing backlogs, delays, and systemic corruption. As shown in many Gallup polls, this has generated a complete distrust of the system by the private sector and the public in general (Buscaglia, Ratliff, and Dakolias 1995). Moreover, the judiciary can also affect the behavior of private investment. In the absence of an impartial and efficient judiciary, the performance of mutually beneficial transactions depends on preexisting reputations and transactions among parties that already know each other. Lacking those, uncertainty hampers the development of many potentially beneficial transactions involving previously unfamiliar parties or startup businesses.

Legal principles supporting the prevailing economic systems in many developing countries are usually nominally based on the exercise of individual property rights and the enforcement of contractual obligations. But legislation is meaningless without an effective judicial system to interpret and apply it. Consistent interpretation and application of the laws provides a stable institutional environment in which the long-term consequences of economic decisions can be assessed by businesses and the public. In this context, an ideal judicial system is composed of institutions capable of applying and interpreting laws equitably, efficiently, and thus effectively. Under most of the judicial systems in developing countries, however, laws are not subject to predictable interpretation. This uncertainty, coupled with delays in resolving cases, further increases the cost of access to justice and doing business.

JUDICIAL SYSTEMS IN DEVELOPING COUNTRIES

The belief is growing that the judicial sector in developing countries is ill-prepared to foster private sector development within a market system. Business surveys conducted by the World Bank (1993 and 1999) indicate that the lack of a judicial system is seen as the third most significant constraint to private sector development after inflation and the absence of basic infrastructure. Critical elements of an efficient judicial system include relatively

TABLE 3

CHANGE IN DELAY IN CIVIL FIRST-INSTANCE
COURTS IN DEVELOPING COUNTRIES,
1973–97

Country	Percent Change in Median Delay	
	1973–85	1986–97
Argentina	18.3%	32.1%
Brazil	4.4	38.1
Chile	10.2	3.2
Colombia	5.7	18.3
Ghana	2.1	25.1
Philippines	4.2	11.4
Mexico	n/a	10.8
Poland	n/a	7.3
Singapore	17.3	6.9
Venezuela	7.4	28.2

predictable outcomes within the courts; accessibility to the courts by the population, regardless of income level; reasonable time to disposition; and adequate court-provided remedies.

Increasing delays, backlogs, and the uncertainty associated with expected court outcomes have diminished the quality of justice from Mexico to China. The judiciary faces several obstacles, including a dysfunctional administration of justice, lack of transparency, and a perception and often reality of systemic corruption. Table 3 shows the average annual percentage increase in delays and backlogs in federal jurisdictions over time in a representative sample of developing countries with reliable data (Buscaglia, Ratliff, and Dakolias 1995; Buscaglia and Dakolias 1999). As we can see, average annual percentage changes during the 1986–97 period show a pronounced deterioration compared to the period 1973–85, which helps explain the public's dissatisfaction with judicial systems throughout the region. Those data may also explain why surveys of the judicial systems in developing countries conducted by the World Economic Forum (in 1993 and 1996) show the majority of potential court users are "not inclined" to bring disputes to court because the systems are perceived as slow, uncertain, and costly or of "poor quality."

One main premise within the economic analysis of the law is that institutions convey implicit prices depending on the type of behavior. For example, if one engages in fraudulent activities, the law through the courts will apply a specific penalty that in part can be translated into monetary terms. An empirical analysis must identify the extent to which the prices imposed by legal procedures change the court users' behavior. For instance, Buscaglia (1996) shows that the court system increases the cost of resolving disputes when times to disposition increase. This study shows that the yearly percentage growth in the time-to-court dispositions faced by the general public in selected developing countries have been increasing since 1990, which brings an increase in the average cost of litigation. Under these conditions of rising time and costs, people reduce their filings and thus do not redress their grievances within the court system. Buscaglia's (1996) results also confirm the account of the informal courts of justice given by de Soto (1989) in Peru, where people quit the formal court system and resolve their disputes within neighborhood councils. A judicial crisis is identified with precision for the first time in the literature in Buscaglia (1996) and Buscaglia, Ratliff, and Dakolias (1995). Specifically, a judicial crisis begins at the point where backlogs, delays, and payoffs increase the cost (implicit or explicit) of accessing the system. When costs become too high, people start restricting their use of the judiciary. The collapse of most developing countries' judiciaries takes place in the complete absence of legally enforced alternative dispute resolution mechanisms (e.g., arbitration or mediation).

As stated above, recent surveys of the region's judicial systems indicate that the majority of court users are "not inclined" to bring disputes to court. This lack of confidence in the administration of justice is more pronounced among small economic units and low-income families. For example, about 55 percent of business-court users surveyed in Latin America responded that they prefer to negotiate a partial settlement rather than adjudicating in the formal court system (Buscaglia, Ratliff, and Dakolias 1995), perhaps also because clerks and judges are often poorly trained due to the lack of specialized or continuing education programs for court officers in commercial, tax, and other business-related matters. As a result, judges are forced to rely on nonlegal experts for resolving business and commercial cases. Additionally, the common use of ex parte communication throughout Latin America contributes to the public perception of corrupt behavior. Under ex parte communication, parties can approach judges and judges can request to see the parties in a case or their lawyers separately. Court users often feel that cases are decided in these meetings. The problems associated with ex parte communication are compounded by an insufficient number of prosecutors and publicly funded defense attorneys. The view of individuals and businesses alike is that corrupt practices are required in order to motivate court personnel, including judges, to process cases that otherwise may stay pending for years (Buscaglia 1998b).

The enhancement of the capability of the courts to satisfy the people's demand for justice is a challenging and important aspect of judicial reform in developing countries. As we saw in table 3, courts are unable to supply enough services to satisfy the current demand. Delays can be attributed to a lack of resources or procedural defects on the supply side and vagueness in the application of the law causing excessive litigiousness on the demand side (Buscaglia and Ulen 1997). For example, some argue that many countries in the developing world provide inadequate budgets to the courts, which prevents the judiciary from providing even minimal public access to justice. Inadequate budgets, then, perpetuate the dependence of the judiciary on the executive and the legislative branches, generate corruption among court personnel, and prevent the judiciary from attracting well-qualified judges and support staff. Thus many judges and legal scholars argue that the judiciary must have a separate budget that it proposes and manages (Buscaglia, Ratliff, and Dakolias 1995).

Of course, it is essential that the judiciary be provided with an adequate budget so that it can offer competitive merit-based salaries to its personnel and attract well-qualified lawyers to the bench. On average, salaries remain low as compared to other private sector nonprofit jobs. For example, in Ecuador and Venezuela, judges' real salaries have increased threefold while support staffs' real salaries have increased 54 percent. Yet compensation is still low in comparison to lawyers' salaries in nonprofit agencies. The same is true in Argentina and Uganda where real salary levels in their federal systems remain unattractive (Buscaglia 1998b).

As a way to resolve these problems, some developing countries have proposed allotting a prespecified proportion of the governments' budget to the judiciary not only as a way to address the low-salary problem but also as a mechanism to reduce times to disposition and backlogs. But a country-by-country approach is always required. Because of international differences in procedural requirements, substantive law, and cultural legal history, the resources needed by courts to produce a certain type and quantity of services (e.g., 1,000 bankruptcy rulings) will greatly vary among countries (Buscaglia 1996). This means that, for example, 10 percent of one county's budget allocated to the judiciary may have a very different impact on times to disposition and court productivity in another country. In fact, the people in countries that do not have serious problems with delays and corruption, such as Denmark, Japan, Germany, the Netherlands, and Norway, have a high degree of public satisfaction or confidence in their judiciary. But these countries devote a smaller portion of their annual budgets to the judiciary than developing countries such as Argentina, Brazil, Uganda, and Nigeria, which are in the bottom 20 percent of the public's confidence (Buscaglia and Dakolias 1999). Therefore, there is no proven significant international correlation between judicial efficiency (measured in terms of backlogs and times to disposition) and the size of a government's budget allocated to the courts. This is true for a number of reasons, again ranging from culture to more easily measured factors. One explanation may be that under the best of circumstances additional resources (personnel and capital) are likely to initially reduce backlogs and delay because of greater court productivity. But after some time, a more efficient judiciary starts expanding the demand for justice from citizens and businesses who had previously been reluctant to use the courts. The joint effects of both forces make it difficult to determine the consequences of solely adding or subtracting resources devoted to the judiciary. It is therefore much more sensible to implement a budgetary mechanism whereby courts can request funds based on projected increases in filings within each subject matter and geographic jurisdiction (Buscaglia 1996).

Given the lack of a strong correlation between court productivity and increases in resources, other factors affecting the supply of court services, such as excessive administrative burdens falling on judges, must also be considered. For example, Buscaglia and Dakolias (1995) and Buscaglia (1999) have found that between 60 and 70 percent of Argentine, Ecuadorian, Ugandan, and Venezuelan judges' time is spent on nonadjudicative tasks dealing with administrative issues, such as signing checks or requesting office supplies. Moreover, between 20 and 40 percent of the court officers interviewed seem to welcome administrative tasks (Buscaglia and Dakolias 1995), perhaps because administrative duties give judges a false sense of budgetary autonomy and bureaucratic power.

Many factors may help explain low court productivity (i.e., low supply of services) in developing countries. These factors include the lack of court resources devoted to capital spending, the lack of an effective case management style, and an excessive amount of time devoted to court administrative procedures by judges and clerks (Buscaglia and Ulen 1997). Low court productivity may also be due to court personnel lacking (1) a clear conception of the courts' mission (i.e., resolution of conflicts); (2) efficient organizational strategies to accomplish their mission (e.g., knowing the optimal case management style for a judge); (3) methods of evaluation, such as quantifiable measures of how well the court has accomplished its mission; and (4) quality control techniques applied to procedural times. Any organization, private or public, must incorporate these four factors into the activities of its administrative and jurisdictional personnel if it wishes to experience a high level of productivity and user satisfaction. The implementation of these reforms, however, requires flexibility in the allocation of budget resources to each court because the court personnel's compensation and tenure should be linked to professional performance. Flexible compensation coupled with managerial quality control could promote the incentives needed to increase the productivity of court personnel. All these elements are currently absent in all judicial systems in most developing countries except Chile, Costa Rica, and Singapore (Buscaglia 1999; Buscaglia, Ratliff, and Dakolias 1995).

In his book *The Mystery of Capital* (forthcoming), Hernando de Soto explains how the developed Western nations went through many of the same problems as the developing world today. Ultimately, he said, taking the United States as an example, "American politicians expressed the revolutionary idea that legal institutions can survive only if they respond to social needs. . . . Entrepreneurship triumphed in the West because the law integrated everyone under one system of property, giving them the means to cooperate and produce large amounts of surplus value in an expanded market."

CASE STUDY: ECONOMIC AND STATISTICAL ANALYSIS OF THE COURTS IN ARGENTINA AND VENEZUELA

This section identifies and describes the factors affecting the capacity of Argentina and Venezuela to supply court services. Specifically, we address the supply- and demand-related factors that affected procedural times in 190 commercial litigations in Argentina and Venezuela during the mid-1990s. These factors include the lack of court resources, the case management style used by judges, and the time judges and clerks devote to the courts' administrative procedures. We then examine the relationship among these and other factors and the times to disposition of commercial cases in business-related litigation. If public policies in judicial reforms are to be effective, they must employ this kind of pinpoint analysis.

In each country we focused on the Federal District Commercial Courts of First Instance during the 1993–97 period. Interviews were conducted with eighteen judges and 180 court users of nineteen courts in the two countries. We determined the time it took for disposition of each of the 190 litigations, focusing on the most common areas of commercial litigation in the two countries: bankruptcy, debt collection, and breach of contract.[1] We then examined the supply- and demand-related factors explained above

---

1. For more details on the methodology followed here, see Buscaglia and Ulen (1997).

and determined their correlation with procedural times. For example, costs paid by the users of the court can be direct (court and attorneys' fees, etc.) or indirect (transportation costs, financial costs, loss of workers' time). These expenses are an incentive or disincentive to use the courts and therefore have an impact on the procedural times.

To pinpoint the factors related to the times to disposition, we first need to explain the current imbalance between the demand for and supply of court services. The efficiency of the judiciary is determined by the interplay of supply- and demand-related forces. Standard efficiency measures include the proportion of all cases filed that are annually disposed (i.e., clearance rate), the number of cases decided per judge, the time to disposition, and the cost per case processed. To balance equity and efficiency considerations in the provision of court services, however, a high clearance rate (i.e., high court productivity) must be accompanied by the public's perception of an accessible and high-quality court system. It is possible to find court systems with very high clearance rates that at the same time lack the public's confidence and, therefore, provide a low-quality service.

Previous studies have shown that the question of how to increase court productivity (e.g., decrease times to disposition and increase clearance rates) is an extremely complex issue. This previous research, however, has been based on aggregate case data, such as total cases pending, rather than case-specific information. In contrast, Buscaglia and Ulen (1997) and Buscaglia and Dakolias (1996) analyzed by collecting extensive and detailed information about the litigants, the case structure, and processing practices within the courts.

FACTORS RELATING TO COURT PRODUCTIVITY

We observed that Argentine and Venezuelan courts are both affected by the supply- and demand-related factors noted above.[2] These factors affect productivity measured in terms of the average

2. This section is based on Edgardo Buscaglia and Thomas Ulen, "An Economic Analysis of the Efficiency of the Judicial Sector in Latin America," *International Review of Law and Economics* 17 (4): 314–32 (1997).

procedural times taken by judges to rule in commercial cases as well as the clearance rate. For instance, on the demand side, we see that, as the filings per court increase, it takes significantly longer for a typical commercial case to be ruled on by a judge; that is, the procedural time for the typical case increases. On the supply side, when one considers the productivity effect of adding more resources to the court, such as more court personnel, then the procedural times for an average commercial case will tend to decrease in the short run and the clearance rate (i.e., number of rulings as a proportion of cases filed) will increase. In the longer term, however, for reasons mentioned above, the relationship between adding more resources devoted to personnel and court productivity is insignificant. Another important supply-related factor is the judges' using a modern case management style supported by information technology. This increases productivity and shows that procedural times are not just associated with an increase in resource availability but also to a different use of previously available resources.

We also see that the decrease in the complexity of a case (measured, for example, through the total number of expert witnesses needed) and the greater use of computer technology have a predictable beneficial effect on increasing court productivity. For instance, computer technology is often a useful tool for developing a legal database, for a case-tracking system, and word processing. In our sample of ten courts in Argentina and nine in Venezuela, only 25 percent have computer technology. Yet even this limited use has significantly reduced times to disposition. Another supply-related factor affecting productivity is the training and education of court personnel. Our sample shows that, as the number of years of accumulated education and training devoted to a judge and clerk increases, their productivity (i.e., clearance rates) also tends to increase. Court productivity and effectiveness are reduced by an excessively formalistic legal procedure coupled with low levels of court administration and case-management capability. Formal hearings are rare in commercial cases, and the courts of first instance serve primarily as depositories of documentary evidence that is studied by a judge who is responsible for making determinations of both fact and law.

Filings per court are not the only demand-related factor affecting court productivity. Rather, as the direct and indirect costs paid by users to the courts increase, the number of cases entering the average court decreases. Moreover, our sample of commercial cases shows that the capacity to litigate seems partially determined by the size of the firm involved. More specifically, smaller firms tend to seek an earlier resolution to their litigation than larger firms because the costs impose a heavier burden on their assets and business operations.

In short, an important part of the conclusions driven by recent case studies, found in Buscaglia (1999), Buscaglia and Ulen (1997), and Buscaglia and Ratliff (1997), is that higher salaries have no significant effect on productivity. Instead, greater productivity, and therefore access to justice, must be accomplished through improvements in case-management techniques, a uniform, less time-consuming, and more flexible administrative approach.

POLICY RECOMMENDATIONS IN JUDICIAL REFORMS

If judiciaries are to serve the interests of nations and not just privileged individuals, basic reforms are essential. Although the process will not be easy, as Buscaglia, Ratliff, and Dakolias (1995) have argued, many things can be done to move in the right direction. To be both desirable and successful, the reforms will have to take into account (1) the present and future costs and benefits of reforms to society and (2) the present and future individual benefits (rents) as perceived by affected court officers in particular and government personnel in general.

The crisis the courts face today makes it likely that a radical program of reform can now be undertaken successfully. But since the contemplated changes will in many cases threaten the interests of those currently in power, they must be taken in stages. An effort should be made to convince those in power that the reforms will benefit the nation, which includes themselves and their families, at least in the medium and long terms. But realistically, many inevitable short-term losers—in the courts but also in the political and economic spheres—are going to resist change. For example, court reforms promoting uniformity, transparency, and accountability in the process of enforcing laws would necessarily diminish the court personnel's capacity to extract illicit payments from the public and private sectors. As a result, the court personnel's expected short-term costs for supporting judicial reform seem much greater than expected long-term benefits. This asymmetry between short-term costs and long-term benefits tends to block judicial reforms and explains why court reforms, which eventually would benefit most segments of society, are often resisted and delayed (Buscaglia 1996). Reformers often will need to cajole and even plot how to overcome both the problems themselves and the resistance from vested interests. This may at times require some degree of "buying off" the "losers," and it certainly will necessitate forming alliances against those who resist change. Buscaglia, Ratliff, and Dakolias (1995) demonstrate that a judicial crisis is needed to break with this vicious circle and thus to successfully enact reforms.

The greatest challenges in undertaking serious, constructive, and successful reforms in the judiciaries of developing countries are institutional inertia and changing the way governments and people think and act. Harrison (1985) goes so far as to argue that, at bottom, "underdevelopment is a state of mind," and an increasing number of analysts from developed and developing countries are inclined to agree. Thus the formula for success or failure in reforms, along with the many economic and other advantages they would help bring about, is in the people, that is, the culture, politics, political culture, and institutions of individual nations (Alford 1995; North 1990; Lubman 1994). The most successful reforms are those growing out of society itself or those that are truly accepted at all levels of society. Acceptance at all levels, and thus successful implementation, often takes a long time. For example, Lubman (1997) writes of China's "long march toward legality" and stresses that creating legal *institutions* is only one step toward creating a legal *system*.

Earlier studies have argued that judicial inertia in enacting reforms stems from uncertainty related to the long-term nature of the benefits of reform, such as improved professional prestige and social recognition. In the past, serious problems with law transplants from

Latin America to China have arisen from the beliefs that transplanting is a fairly simple process and that because a law is on the books in a society it is therefore operative (Alford 1995). But as Potter (1995, 2) notes with particular reference to China, "The norms inherent in much of Western law, whether imposed during the colonial period or adopted later on, were often incompatible with social customs and practices that informed local economic activity." Truly changing popular attitudes toward rights, responsibilities, and lining one's pockets at the public's expense—whether from need or greed—at best will come only gradually. But smaller and significant steps, a few of which are suggested below, can be taken in the meantime.

Among the most serious problems in courts from Latin America to China are delays and backlogs, and both are getting worse. In Latin America the times to disposition have increased 85 percent since 1981, meaning that it often takes many years to conclude a case (Buscaglia, Ratliff, and Dakolias 1995). Chinese officials claim to be making headway against enormous backlogs, even though litigation is still not common in China. Although Chinese courts now handle roughly 3.5 million civil and economic cases annually (Lubman 1997), the Supreme People's Court reported in late 1998 that there is a backlog of nearly a million cases, some dating back to 1949 (He Sheng 1998). In most of the developing world, backlogs and delays are brought on by a lack of resources, procedural defects, inadequate training of court staff, and an excessive administrative burden borne by the judges. The only good thing to be said about such problems is that they have made the existing systems so slow, unreliable, and unacceptable that a point of crisis is being reached, which, as we noted above, may precipitate reforms that would not otherwise be possible.

Actions that can be taken now include conducting serious empirical studies to identify the main bottlenecks in the process. Other reforms that could be undertaken immediately include training and encouraging judges to set a better pace of litigation, though constructive activism is often discouraged or impossible in many parts of the developing world (Buscaglia, Ratliff, and Dakolias 1995; Lubman 1994). Also, establishing a small claims court to take care of cases up to a specified amount, waiving court fees to low-income groups, and permitting class action suits would ease the problems (Buscaglia, Ratliff, and Dakolias 1995; Johnson 1999). To the extent that these changes can be even to some degree implemented, they would reduce delays and provide short-term benefits to judges and courts.

In the long term, courts must be independent of political and other forces in the society. But as noted, there often is little or no support for significant change among court officials. Lubman (1994, 4) writes that in most places "the construction of a national legal system requires strong if benign central power to support the enterprise." Thus in the reform period, independence must often be circumscribed. The central authority may have its own agenda; as Alford (1995, 5) notes, with respect to China, laws and regulations in essence "are enacted explicitly to achieve immediate policy objectives of the regime. In this context, law is not a limit on state power; it is a mechanism by which state power is exercised."

Even so, some things can and should be done to move the courts in the direction of independence. For example, job stability needs to be made the norm, as should higher real salaries and retirement systems, giving those in court greater independence from the political powers that now so often control them. Although more problematical, because they could either strengthen entrenched forces or be utterly rejected by them, there could be greater judicial budget autonomy and more transparent and credible appointment and disciplinary procedures. Legal education is the sine qua non in the development of a just and efficient judiciary. This means education and training for students and lawyers, judicial training for judges, and legal education for the public at large. Curricula and faculty in schools must be improved, and continuing education should be far more accessible. In some parts of the world the problem is inadequate education; in others it is the virtual absence of any training.

Practitioners of the legal profession must be required to achieve and maintain high standards of work. In Latin America, professional guidelines and ethical standards are deliberately vague, as they are in China, where the legal infrastructure is still in the process of formation, which could be turned to China's advantage. But even if guidelines were clearer, there are few mechanisms and often not the will to enforce them. Alford (1995) points to a problem with respect to China that is, as we have said, pervasive in the developing world: too little focus on the empirical evaluation of how laws are working. Lubman (1999) reports that in China legislative practice is in "remarkable disorder, marked by the lack of centralized agencies to interpret legislation and administrative rules and by the continued use of broadly drafted wording that leaves wide scope for bureaucratic discretion." Further, Alford (1999) notes that "Chinese judges suffer from the triple whammy of being drawn almost exclusively from the ranks of the part, lacking independence from the local authorities who pay their salaries and yet finding it hard to secure enforcement of their judgments, whether against the state or other actors."

In Latin America, ex parte communication constantly sows doubts about objectivity in institutions riddled with corruption, favoritism, and inertia. Finally, a variety of problems could be relieved if judicial councils were allowed to exercise their administrative and disciplinary functions. Since many supreme courts and politicians view judicial councils as a threat to their control and perks, strengthening these bodies might be implemented in the context of a package of judicial change that would also deal with some of the problems that concern judges and other court personnel.

CHAPTER 4

Alternative Dispute Resolution Mechanisms and Democracy in Developing Countries

Democracy can be defined as a process wherein interrelated institutional mechanisms translate social preferences into political and economic action (Buscaglia 1996). Examples of this include the translation of social preferences through political parties and civil society's nongovernmental groups (NGOs). Democracy is strengthened when the most effective institutional mechanisms translate social preferences into political results. Three institutional developments—universal franchise, single-district open-list electoral systems, and the gradual emergence of organized constituencies (i.e., civil society)—have made it easier for citizens to hold their elected officials accountable in the process of expressing their social preferences (Transparency International 1998). But we would add that the courts and ADR mechanisms are ways in which individuals are able to redress their grievances whenever their rights are violated. Therefore, interpreting and enforcing laws should be seen as mechanisms that reflect the social preferences of a society when, by a written or unwritten ruling, a court captures the evolving social norms related to conflict resolution (Buscaglia 1996).

This chapter is based on Edgardo Buscaglia and Pilar Domingo, "Political and Economic Impediments to Judicial Reform in Latin America," in *The Law and Economics of Development,* ed. Edgardo Buscaglia, William Ratliff, and Robert Cooter (Greenwich:JAI Press, 1997), 291–312.

Extending Cooter's (1996) conclusions, if a law is poorly adapted to the habits and customs followed by those who interact socially, conflicts are more common, cooperation is more difficult, and ensuing disputes create ill-will and consume resources. Conversely, if law is derived from and adapted to informal codes of conduct, people are much more likely to cooperate with one another, harmonize their expectations, and use resources efficiently and creatively. Cooter and de Soto (forthcoming) argue that efficiency is enhanced by a "bottom-up" process of capturing social norms that are already in place, with norms understood as coordinating mechanisms for social interaction. This decentralized approach to lawmaking stands in sharp contrast to the centralization proposed by the first law and development movement in the 1960s and 1970s (Seidman 1978; Galanter 1974; and Trubek 1972), which sponsored a comprehensive legislative reform program covering the modernization of the public and private dimensions of laws through transplants around the world.

To be sure, the original legal frameworks in many developing countries had been originally transplanted from Europe. For centuries Europeans relied primarily on bottom-up judicial lawmaking under the Roman and later European *jus civile* (civil law), coupled with private sector lawmaking under the *lex mercatoria* (merchant law). But the eighteenth-century Enlightenment brought major changes. The lawyers and judges of the old order were considered personifications of the late monarchy. The then dominant and exaggerated rationalism believed, as Merryman (1985, 28) says, that "history could be abolished by repealing a statute." French and other European revolutionaries wanted future parliaments to make all the laws on the assumption that parliaments were the institutionalization of the social will and thus the best mechanisms to engineer a better and more prosperous society. These laws were to be written down so clearly, coherently, and completely that ordinary people could understand and apply them in their own lives. Judges would apply the law by selecting the applicable provision of the code in hand; they would not be permitted to interpret the law and thereby reintroduce ideas and practices of the past (Merryman 1985; North and

Weingast 1989). The irony was that this centralized approach to lawmaking decreased popular participation. This top-down approach to law, strongly influenced by the French Revolution and within the general framework of the Napoleonic model of centralized parliamentary lawmaking, was later transplanted by colonial powers and/or others to much of the Americas, Africa, and Asia. During the early nineteenth-century independence movement in Latin America, for example, courts were forced to give up their aristocratic roots and depend on parliaments so as to obey the "will of the people." This top-down aspect of governing—which was typical of the indigenous traditions in most cases—survives to this day in most countries and has become increasingly divorced from community level social norms (Cooter 1996). One could thus argue that over time judicial systems have become increasingly undemocratic—or at least not more democratic—due to their failure to draw laws and doctrines on the basis of customs, habits, and general norms of behavior.

Thus, if developing countries aspire to strengthen and consolidate their democratic institutions and economic reforms, they need to develop a legal system that will reflect today's social norms. Such a legal system would allow private citizens to develop their own rules in solving their disputes as long as the public interest is not at stake. In this context, the emergence and expansion of fledgling private dispute resolution mechanisms—such as conciliation, mediation, arbitration, negotiation, and neighborhood councils—reflect a step forward in consolidating democracy.

THE JUDICIAL SYSTEM'S PRESENT FAILURE

With democratization and economic liberalization in developing countries, there has been a renewed interest in institutional and public sector reforms. As explained above, democratization, expanding urbanization, and the adoption of market reforms in developing countries have all created additional but unfulfilled demands for court services and the rule of law. These changes have increased the complexity of social interactions, thereby making the improvement of private and public dispute resolution mechanisms ever more necessary. In addition, the shift of most economic trans-actions toward the market domain and away from the public ad-ministrative sphere has created an unprecedented increase in private sector demands for an improved definition of rights and obligations. The failure of the state to reduce backlogs and uncer-tainties is clearly documented in Buscaglia, Ratliff, and Dakolias (1995). What is more, from Argentina to China, judiciaries are weakened by a dysfunctional administration of justice, a lack of transparency, and a presumption of corruption (Blair and Hansen 1994; Lubman 1996). In Argentina, for example, a Gallup poll found that 77 percent of the public believed that judges were cor-rupt. Moreover, as Buscaglia, Ratliff, and Dakolias (1995) show, time delays and corruption within the developing countries' judi-cial systems are reaching unprecedented proportions, despite real and apparent efforts to control them.

The basic elements of an effective judicial system are often miss-ing. These elements are (1) predictable and consistent dispute res-olution and enforcement capabilities; (2) access to the courts for nonfrivolous actions by the people regardless of their income level; and (3) efficient provision of court services based on rea-sonable times to disposition, adequate remedies, and acceptable quality standards (Buscaglia and Guerrero 1997).

The problems with present court services often make alternative mechanisms to solve their conflicts all the more desirable. In fact, as Goldsmith (1993, 414, 416) remarks, the ADR solution was "born out of crisis" and, when functioning, "permits the speedy resolution of numerous complex commercial disputes which have been bogged down in a legal swamp after years of fruitless and costly confronta-tion." This is particularly appropriate in many parts of the devel-oping world, including Africa and Asia, which have long traditions of resolving problems through some form of compromise. Indeed, a major Western/Chinese law firm operating in China in the late 1990s warns that "One litigates . . . only if there is little chance of collecting the debt by other means" (L&L 1998). Today, more and more "other means," namely, formal and government-authorized private and public ADR mechanisms, have emerged in some devel-oping countries to redress domestic and sometimes international grievances in a more timely, consistent, and, in many cases, honest manner than is possible in official courts.

By reducing the state courts' discretionary power and breaking their monopoly over the provision of conflict resolution, ADR channels enhance the disputing parties' control over the process of seeking consensual solutions. That is, the more generalized use of ADR mechanisms—arbitration, mediation, conciliation, and negotiation—has the potential to limit corrupt practices and enhance access to justice for those marginalized sectors of the population who are not able or willing to pay an illicit price for court services.

ALTERNATIVE DISPUTE RESOLUTION MECHANISMS: ADVANTAGES AND DISADVANTAGES

Clearly, the increasing demand for justice in the developing world has not been matched by an increase in the supply of court services. A number of factors have blunted the incentives of the region's judiciaries to solve disputes effectively and to make their services available to the large segments of the population that now lack access to them. High among such factors is an unwillingness to give up the remunerative corrupt practices facilitated by, among other things, the absence of any or significant competition from ADRs. Therefore, most developing countries continue to have maladjusted judicial systems at a time when the nature and scope of social interaction have changed dramatically due to emerging demographic, technological, economic, and political forces that have increased the demand for legal services. Since access to the courts has been inadequate, the public in general and businesses in particular have had to find other means to solve disputes. These circumstances account for the growing presence of public (i.e., court-annexed) and private alternative mechanisms aimed at solving conflicts. For example, public mediation mechanisms composed of court-appointed mediators represent a laboratory within the courts where formulas to reduce caseloads and procedural times are being experimented with. At the same time, private mechanisms have the potential to expand the marketplace of judicial options and allow disputing parties to seek their own solutions in ways that reflect their own social norms and practices. For example, in Argentina today both public and private ADRs deal with family law (marriage and divorce), collective and individual labor conflicts, legislation on automobile and property titles, cooperative real estate, neighborhood conflicts, and real estate rent disputes. These cases taken together make up 78 percent of the nation's total ADR caseload. In El Salvador and Uganda, in contrast, public ADR programs are designed to respond specifically to land title disputes. Since the early 1980s, Hong Kong has accepted arbitration to settle domestic and international disputes (a high percentage of them dealing with construction), and O'Hare (1996) expects Hong Kong to become the "premier Asian arbitration center" by about 2005. The China International Economic and Trade Arbitration Commission accepted nearly a thousand Sino-foreign disputes in 1996 and, according to Lubman (1997), is "now the world's busiest international arbitration organization" with "a good reputation internationally" (Lubman 1993).

MOST-COMMON PRIVATE ADR CHANNELS

Private ADR channels are usually offered outside the court system, without state monitoring or permission, and include the following:

Negotiation   This is the first step taken by the parties in conflict. Even before any type of formal dispute resolution starts, the parties listen to each other and identify common interests while defining a consensual solution to their conflict.

Conciliation   In this process, a third party communicates separately with each side in a dispute. The parties try to agree on common interests and concerns linked to the dispute. In a considerable number of cases, a conflict is resolved at this stage.

Mediation   This is an informal and confidential mechanism of dispute resolution where the parties choose a neutral third party who, offering his or her service on a profit or nonprofit basis, assists in the search for mutual interests, areas of agreement, and alternative solutions. The parties engage in conversations and private meetings with the mediator until they find a consensus within the range of solutions proposed. The mediator does not impose the solution and remains neutral throughout the process.

Arbitration   This is usually a service provided by organizations on a nonprofit basis. Here the two sides in a dispute choose a third party to determine the facts of the case and generate a decision. The decision can be binding or nonbinding, depending on the parties' preference, which is agreed on before the arbitrator's final decision. A binding decision avoids further proceedings and reduces conflict-related costs; a nonbinding decision has the advantage of providing a guide for bringing the parties closer to agreement later.

Mediation-Arbitration "Combo"   The parties seek a private mediator working on a nonprofit basis. If they do not reach an agreement, an arbitrator takes over and pursues a resolution to the conflict.

Neighborhood Panels   Panels composed of prestigious volunteers from a neighborhood provide mediation and conciliation services to members of the community.

Most-Common Court-Annexed ADR Mechanisms

Court-Ordered Arbitration   Here the judge orders that the case be heard before an arbitration panel, and the court manages the ADR proceedings. This is common in commercial and labor disputes where money damages are involved.

Court-Ordered Mediation   Judiciaries in Argentina and other countries have a judge determine that public mediation services (approved and regulated by the judiciary or Ministry of Justice) need to be applied to the dispute under consideration.

Early Neutral Evaluation   In these cases, the disputants usually hire a neutral third party early in the process. The official evaluator studies the evidence presented by the parties, listens to witnesses, reads written statements, and meets the disputants with or

without their attorneys. The evaluator then suggests possible av-
enues to agreement based on his or her perception of possible consensus, the substantive merits of the case, and the common ground
that has emerged from the exchange of information. If settlement
fails, the evaluator proposes a plan for sharing information that
may serve to shorten the subsequent procedures.

Voluntary Settlement Conference   This process is similar to early
neutral evaluation in terms of its goals and mechanisms. However,
it takes place at any stage of the conflict and court proceedings.

Minitrials   This is the most common ADR channel adopted in
corporate disputes. Without their lawyers, the parties meet with a
mock judge and state their positions and interests. They later identify business solutions to their dispute and allow the mock judge to
issue an opinion based on the business-related merits of their case.

   In developing countries today, state-sponsored legal procedures
are allowed for public mediation in civil cases. For example, in
Ecuador codes permit judges to encourage settlement discussions
with the parties and mediation services right after a case is filed.
Court-annexed ADR is offered, authorized, and used by the courts
in a number of developing countries, among them Argentina,
Colombia, Costa Rica, Ecuador, Kazakhstan, Kenya, Uganda, and
Singapore. Participation may be voluntary, as in Uganda and
Uruguay, or mandated by the courts, as in Argentina. Decisions in
mediations are nonbinding on the parties, however, which means
that even if the parties come to an agreement they are not prohib-
ited from returning to the formal court system. This process raises
the question of efficiency because ADRs sometimes simply add
one more layer to the conflict resolution process. Yet evidence generally suggests that time, funds, and tempers often are saved by
the use of ADRs. Uruguay, which experimented with public ADR
mechanisms as early as the late 1970s, found that some 60 percent
of legal actions were settled during conciliation hearings; of those,
85 percent were settled because the defendant realized that the
plaintiff had a valid claim (Cappelletti and Garth 1978). More
recent experiments have shown high success rates as well.

Observations at a mediation center set up in Argentina in 1993 show that when parties have asymmetrical expectations of winning a case, early exchanges of information can prevent delays (Buscaglia 1996). Finally, in Colombia, all labor and most civil, traffic, administrative, and family disputes must go through the ADR process of conciliation before a court case is initiated.

ADRs can both supplement the formal court systems in developing countries and, in some respects, offer advantages over them because disputing parties often can sidestep the delays and corruption of the formal judicial system. In fact, though many judges initially feel threatened by ADR options, by reducing delays and backlogs, the mechanisms help court personnel to regain their professional prestige. In addition, ADRs can remove complex and highly visible cases from the courts' dockets.

ADR mechanisms have some clear advantages over the formal court system. Well-trained mediators and arbitrators can provide more specialized knowledge of a specific kind of dispute than judges and therefore may provide more predictable outcomes than courts. Also, public and private ADR mechanisms enjoy a comparative advantage over the formal courts in many cases. For example, ADR mechanisms have the advantage when disputing parties (1) want to maintain a future relationship that going to court might make difficult because of the more aggressive nature of litigation; (2) wish to play a more active role in resolving their dispute due to the confidential nature of the conflict; (3) prefer to talk directly to each other in cases with low transaction costs (i.e., low costs of acquiring information) and low communication costs; or (4) interact in a market where a specific conflict is not uncommon (e.g., credit card companies).

In some cases, the disadvantages of litigation may provide the most important reason for deciding to use ADR mechanisms. Among the most common disadvantages of solving a dispute through the official courts are the length of time to decide the case, the direct cost of court-related services (attorney fees, court fees, and even bribes), and the emotional strain imposed by the confrontation inherent in litigation. Also, with litigation the parties may have to spend time with their attorney explaining their desires

and concerns, and even then the parties may lose control over the
case to their attorneys. A judge ignorant of the circumstances may
have to be educated by the parties themselves so that she or he will
not base her or his decision on procedural rules rather than the
merits of the case.

In most developing countries, private ADR assistance for commercial disputes is often offered by chambers of commerce,
though they are seldomly used because of their high cost. In contrast, justices of the peace elected by the communities or
appointed by the judicial system are widely accepted in many
countries (Brandt 1991), including Peru and Uganda. Justices of
the peace often have little or no formal training in resolving disputes but keep proposing solutions until the parties agree. Their
decisions or proposed solutions may not be based on legal foundations, however, and thus they are frequently appealed, though
some countries have created well-functioning systems of justices
of the peace where cases are seldomly appealed.

In short, a review of the literature points to seven major potential comparative advantages of public and private alternative dispute mechanisms in developing countries over the formal public
court system. Such ADR mechanisms have the potential to

1.   Reduce the unbearable caseload found in most courts
(Edwards 1986).

2.   Increase access of marginalized groups to publicly recognized and sometimes binding solutions to their conflicts
(Houseman 1993).

3.   Permit a less corrupt and more predictable forum because
of the lack of discretionary power in the hands of the courts
(Buscaglia 1996).

4.   Lower the direct and indirect costs of solving disputes
(Johnson 1993).

5.   Provide a laboratory for public courts where innovative
procedural and managerial formulas can be experimented with,
even as they reduce case loads and times to disposition (Ippolito
1990).

6.   Expand the resolution options available to the public and businesses (Spain 1994).

7.   Most important, reduce present and future transaction costs by creating a channel through which the evolution of social norms and business practices can be incorporated into the resolution of disputes.

Quantitative analysis presented by Buscaglia (1998a) supports the cost advantage of public ADR within family and commercial cases in Ecuador. Moreover, the experience of Ecuador shows that low-income groups have in fact taken substantial advantage of this greater access to justice through ADR mechanisms.

PUBLIC VERSUS PRIVATE ADR: ADVANTAGES AND DISADVANTAGES

ADR mechanisms are being increasingly adopted in and adapted for developing countries under court-annexed and private modes (Buscaglia, Ratliff, and Dakolias 1995). Yet state involvement through the regulation of ADR can hamper its aforementioned comparative advantages. For example, mandatory court-annexed mediation (as in Argentina), the imposition of entry requirements for private organizations offering ADR services (Colombia), or the imposition of regulated requirements within the mediation process (Colombia and Singapore) all can hamper the comparative advantages of ADR. The developing-country experience with court-annexed ADR indicates that, when a judge imposes a conciliator or mediator on the parties, it does not provide the proper incentive for the parties to be candid about the case (Buscaglia 1998b). Frequently, such ADR advantages as procedural flexibility, low cost, enhanced access for marginalized groups, and a predictable forum for dispute resolution tend to disappear when there is discretionary power in the hands of court personnel, procedural formalities within the mediation process, or an artificial limit to competition within the ADR market. One major and underlying rationale for adopting private ADR mechanisms in the first place is to bypass a corrupt judicial system, and a regulated public ADR mechanism, with its increased prospects for abuse by court personnel and excessive legal fees, misses the point.

Private ADR is currently offered in many countries on a for-profit and nonprofit basis. There is, however, a widely held misconception in developing countries that for-profit services diminish the probity and sense of fairness required from a third-party evaluator of a conflict. Some argue that money and justice should not mix. Establishing an ADR center is a labor-intensive enterprise, however, and costs must be paid. Because the fixed cost is low (Burs 1996), however, entry barriers to the ADR market are low, and, barring state-sponsored quotas or regulatory constraints, competition is bound to be intense. Under these competitive conditions the for-profit ADR supplier can be expected to have a strong interest in maintaining a high-level reputation.

For this to work, information about individual ADR providers should be made readily available to the public through specialized agencies with the capacity to assess the quality of the ADR providers. One rationale for market failures is that consumers do not have perfect information regarding the quality of the products they purchase. In some cases, consumers may be able to monitor the overall quality of services as a group but not the quality and risk associated with particular ADR providers. In situations where disputants know the average quality and risk associated with ADR services in general, but not the quality of individual providers, disputants will make their judgments based on the average quality found across the entire market. The losers, when people use this "across-the-market" measurement, are the high-quality ADR services (i.e., the providers reaching the highest settlement rates reflecting the consensus between the disputants), and the winners are the low-quality ADR providers. Thus the presence of group-based pricing provides a disincentive for ADR providers at the high end of the market because their efforts to improve quality will not be rewarded. Therefore, to assure the constant improvement and monitoring of quality standards, ADR private associations, such as ones found in Colombia, must exist and be required to generate and publicize information related to the quality of their service based on the periodical assessment of disputants. This private association (à la Standard and Poor's in the United States) must also establish a code of ethics and create disciplinary panels with the authority to bar from the market those ADR providers infringing on the commonly accepted ethical rules.

For-profit ADR providers must also be willing and able to supply the same ADR services to those disputants who do not have the means to pay the market price for the service. A disputant who falls below a minimum income level (defined as poverty) must be entitled to a state-issued voucher that the disputant can use to hire the ADR provider of choice. Then, both low- and high-income disputants will have the same opportunity to choose a high-quality ADR provider.

In the absence of any other guarantor of justice, the need to introduce generally accepted private mechanisms to solve disputes within marginalized communities has become increasingly urgent. Most people have long preferred to solve their disputes privately within communities and informal groups. But in recent years there has been a rapid increase in criminal cases, where previous methods are not applicable or don't work, and thus communities have taken matters into their own hands. This has brought an increase in vigilantism, mob justice, and lynchings. For example, in Argentina, Ecuador, and Kenya there has been an unprecedented increase in the number of informal community-imposed corporal punishments related to criminal actions. In all these cases due process was lacking and human rights violations were committed in increasing numbers (Buscaglia 1996). This again highlights the increasing divorce between the formal legal system and the mechanisms used by people to solve their conflicts on a daily basis.

To sum up, the development of private ADR channels is needed in order to help avoid (1) the discretionary powers of the courts and therefore corruption shifting to the public ADR system; (2) the imitation of the formal procedures found in public courts within the public ADR process; (3) the artificial limits to competition imposed by regulations on private organizations providing court-annexed ADR; and (4) a worsening in the caseload and time delay experienced within the public court system.

Finally, the legalization and promotion of for-profit private ADR will create pressure for improvements within the formal public ADR system. By forcing the public system to compete and by encouraging improvements in its training and management practices, public ADR will tend to become more efficient. Moreover, private ADR promotes an institutional mechanism to incorporate the community's perception of what is right or fair in a specific time and region. In this way, the public sector's ADR capacity to imitate the conciliation techniques, procedural guidelines, and resolutions found in private ADR mechanisms would tend to decentralize certain areas of the legal system. Therefore, public backing of private ADR resolutions has the potential to transfer the informal or indigenous social norms into the public ADR system. In this way, private ADR would provide an additional democracy-strengthening channel in which the evolution of social preferences and norms could be incorporated into the legal arena. This incorporation of norms into laws would be implicitly made by judges who are familiar with ADR proceedings and solutions and can thus reinterpret statutes in the future in a way that is compatible with the present evolution of social norms and practices.

ADR MECHANISMS: USE AND RECOMMENDED SCOPE

So far there is no study in the literature providing a framework within which we can determine the case types that should be treated within the ADR domain. At present, judges are willing to allocate a dispute to a public ADR forum if the case is causing backlogs in the court system or demands excessive court resources. Historically, courts have used mediation and conciliation for family cases, especially alimony and divorce, and in commercial and labor disputes. Cases of spousal abuse are sometimes excluded from mediation programs because of the imbalance of power between the victim and the accused. Yet in Argentina since 1993 and in Uganda since 1994 many cases involving domestic violence have been sent to mediation centers with mixed results (Buscaglia 1998b). In general, cases where parties hold unequal power are not recommended for mediation, negotiation, or conciliation. However, arbitration may provide a mechanism that can successfully deal with the imbalance of power. Some countries use arbitration for collective or individual labor disputes, domestic violence, or commercial disputes between firms of unequal size and market power.

Smaller economic units rely on negotiations but not to the same extent as larger enterprises. Some lawyers who represent smaller entities feel that they are not as familiar with the technique of negotiation, which leads them to rely more often on the formal court system (Buscaglia 1995). Yet, unlike the established producers, new firms face credit constraints and therefore cannot afford the economic consequences of delay and the illicit payments needed for procedural speed within the courts. In this context, when new firms do not have enough cash to pay bribes and cannot raise the funds because of the lack of collateral, they are deterred from entering the market unless they find a forum for potential dispute resolution that can neutralize differences in negotiating power and experience. Private arbitration offers a potential solution for a small firm's plight in situations where unequal market power is present during a legal dispute with a larger firm.

Private and public mediation share the advantage of preserving the future relationship between the parties in dispute after the proceedings have been concluded. However, in order for mediation or conciliation to be effective, the perceived prior costs of gathering information related to their dispute cannot be high. Mediation requires the parties to identify the common interest during the settlement of their dispute. For this common interest to be identified, the communication, information, and monitoring costs of future behavior cannot be excessive.

The main disadvantage of ADR mechanisms is the absence of precedent. The parties' consensual solution by mediation or the decision of an arbitrator does not serve as a legal precedent for other decision makers facing similar cases in the future. This eliminates the *immediate* emergence of a precedent or doctrine in all ADR mechanisms that could serve in all future similar conflicts. Therefore, when the substance of a conflict involves constitutional issues (e.g., civil/political liberties), international human rights, competition rules, or administrative law, ADR mechanisms will not generate immediate resolutions. In these cases, the public court system is needed as the only mechanism able to supply a public good in the form of doctrines to be enforced by the coercive power of the state. Thus ADR mechanisms should be used only when the substance of a dispute does not involve matters where the coercive power of the state must be exercised. This would exclude from ADR consideration cases involving civil rights, political liberties, administrative law, national security, and organized crime, among others.

CHAPTER 5

Economic Analysis of Systemic Official Corruption

As explained in the previous chapters, the law and economics of development focus on the effects that well-functioning legal and judicial systems have on economic efficiency and development. Adam Smith states in his *Lectures on Jurisprudence* that a factor that "greatly retarded commerce was the imperfection of the law and the uncertainty in its application" (Smith 1978, 528). Entrenched corrupt practices within the public sector (i.e., official systemic corruption) hamper the clear definition and enforcement of laws, and, therefore, as Smith would say, commerce is impeded.

Systemic corruption within the public sector can be defined as the systematic use of public office for private benefit, resulting in a reduction in the quality or availability of government-provided goods and services (Buscaglia 1997). Corruption is systemic when a government agency only supplies a good or service if an unwilling and uncompensated transfer of wealth takes place between the market and the public sector (e.g., bribery, extortion, fraud, or embezzlement).

Rose-Ackerman (1997, 5) states that "widespread corruption is a symptom that the state is functioning poorly." Many other studies have also shown that the presence of perceived corruption retards economic growth, lowers investment, decreases private savings, and hampers political stability (Mauro 1995; Shleifer and

Vishny 1993). Moreover, foreign direct investment has demonstrated a special negative reaction to the presence of corruption within the public sectors in developing countries (Leiken 1996).

Studies describing corrupt practices and analyzing the impact of corruption on economic development are abundant. Low compensation of employees and weak monitoring systems are generally considered the main causes of corruption. (Nadelmann 1993). In Becker and Stigler (1974) and Klitgaard (1991), expected corruption through the bribery of public officials reduces the incidence of punishment, which in itself hampers deterrence. When this is the case, increasing the salaries of public enforcers and/or paying private enforcement agencies for performance improves the quality of enforcement.

Rose-Ackerman (1978), Macrae (1982), Shleifer and Vishny (1993), and Mauro (1995) take different approaches to the economic analysis of corruption. In their studies, corruption is a behavioral phenomenon occurring between the state and the market domains. In all cases they assume that, though ethical attitudes matter in the end, to greater and lesser degrees, people and firms respond to incentives and disincentives by perceiving the probability of apprehension and conviction and the severity of punishment (Becker 1993).

The existence of official corruption distorts market operations by introducing uncertainty in social and economic interactions (Andvig 1991). Moreover, corruption in the public domain is an essential factor in the growth of organized criminal groups with the capacity to pose a significant international security threat through illicit traffic in narcotics, nuclear, chemical, and biological materials, as well as international smuggling and money laundering (Leiken 1996). Taking into account the pernicious effect of corruption on economic development, in August 1997 the International Monetary Fund for the first time suspended aid to a country (Kenya), and since that time the presence of systemic corruption has been one of the factors considered at the Fund when granting a loan (McQuillan and Montgomery 1999).

The literature mentioned above provides an outstanding overview of the social situations associated with entrenched corruption within the public sectors. Although the studies cited above have made path-breaking contributions to the economic analysis of corruption, developing reliable anticorruption policies must go beyond an account of the general situations enhancing corrupt practices. In addition, anticorruption strategies require isolating and empirically testing the main legal, organizational, and economic causes of corruption within specific public sector institutions.

This chapter reviews the causes of corruption within the judiciary. If we are to use our analysis to develop public policy prescriptions in the fight against government corruption, we must attempt to empirically verify our conclusions. We must consider the private costs to officials when fighting public sector corruption as a significant cause of foot-dragging or institutional inertia in efforts to implement public sector reforms in developing countries.

Additionally, such judicial corruption as paying a bribe to win a case can have a profound impact on the average citizen's perception of social equity and on economic efficiency (Buscaglia 1997). These judgments on how equitable the social environment is also must be considered when calculating the long-term impact of corruption on efficiency.

CAUSES OF AND RESPONSES TO CORRUPTION IN JUDICIARIES

An empirical analysis is essential if one wishes to understand and find a realistic remedy for a political, social, or economic problem. This is particularly true in the case of corruption. Corruption as discussed here is the use of public office for private benefit; systemic corruption is the same but within an organization or institution that will not function without its presence. The probability of detecting corruption decreases as the corruption becomes increasingly systemic, and, therefore, the traditional methods of detection and enforcement become less effective. Under these circumstances, experience has shown that such preventive measures as organizational changes (e.g., reducing procedural complexities in the provision of public services) and salary increases are more effective.

The growth and decline of systemic corruption is also subject to the behavior of groups and individuals. All these factors must be examined empirically before formulating and implementing public policies to reduce or eliminate corruption. Thus we must (1) formulate a policy hypothesis on the basis of existing experience, such as that administrations with high concentrations of organizational power in the hands of fewer public officials are prone to more-corrupt behavior; (2) formulate a logical explanation of why the hypothesis is true; (3) objectively collect information to support or disprove the hypothesis; and (4) when convinced that the proposition is correct, design public policies based on the findings.

To so design public policies in the fight against corruption, it is necessary to build a database with quantitative and qualitative information about the factors that are thought to be related to certain types of systemic corrupt behavior, including embezzlement, bribery, extortion, and fraud. For example, the World Bank is currently assembling a database on judicial systems worldwide (Buscaglia and Gonzalez de Asis forthcoming).*

International experience shows that specific policy actions are associated with the reduction of corruption in countries ranging from Uganda and Singapore to Hong Kong and Chile (Buscaglia 1999). These actions include (1) lowering tariffs and other trade barriers; (2) unifying market exchange and interest rates; (3) eliminating enterprise subsidies; (4) minimizing enterprise regulation, licensing requirements, and other barriers to market entry; (5) privatizing while demonopolizing government assets; (6) enhancing transparency in the enforcement of banking, auditing, and accounting standards; and (7) improving tax and budget administration.

Also needed are civil service reform, legal and judicial reforms, and strengthening and expanding civil and political liberties. Finally, the following factors must be addressed: (1) improving administrative procedures by avoiding discretionary decision making and duplication of functions, while at the same time introducing time- and

---

* The World Bank Institute is currently using this type of analysis in its examination of public sector governance. For more details, see Kaufmann, Kray, and Zoido-Lobaton.

production-related performance standards for all employees; (2) setting salaries on the basis of performance standards; (3) reducing the level of organizational power of individuals in an organization; (4) reducing procedural complexity; and (5) making norms, internal rules, and laws well known among officials and users.

Sequencing Anticorruption Policies

Based on the aforementioned empirical findings, the following steps have been found to be the most effective in designing anticorruption policies:

1.   Identify and prioritize the main institutional areas in the country suffering from systemic corruption. This identification must be conducted through surveys of users of government services, businesspersons, taxpayers, and the like. The survey should treat each government institution (e.g., customs, judiciary, tax agencies, and others).

2.   Once a list of areas subject to systemic corruption is available, develop a database for each institution containing objective and subjective measures of corruption and related information. These include (a) reports of corruption; (b) indictments related to fraud, embezzlement, extortion, or bribery; (c) prices charged by the agency; (d) procedural times in the provision of government services; (e) users' perceptions of efficiency, effectiveness, corruption, and access to the agency; and (f) procedural complexity in the provision of services.

3.   Working with the database, statistically analyze the specific factors causing corruption in each government agency. Determine which economic, institutional, and organizational factors mentioned above are related to corruption.

Once these diagnostic and identification stages are complete, elements of civil society (e.g., chambers of commerce and neighborhood councils) should be brought in to monitor the implementation of anticorruption policies. The action plan aims at finding a consensus between civil society and government on particular problems, solutions, deadlines for implementation of solutions, and expected results. This approach has been applied by an interdisciplinary team consisting of economists, lawyers, sociologists, and political scientists at the municipal levels in Venezuela and within the judiciaries in Chile and Ecuador with encouraging results (Buscaglia and Gonzalez de Asis forthcoming). In these cases, the following steps were followed:

1.   A survey was conducted of those users demanding a service from their local government (county office) or judiciaries. The users, interviewed just after finishing the application procedure, were asked to rank the efficiency, effectiveness, level of access, quality of the information received, and corruption they had experienced in the administrative procedures followed.

2.   Numerical and qualitative data gathered to identify the variables affecting the public's responses to the survey were statistically analyzed.

3.   The results of this diagnostic study were then evaluated at a workshop with representatives of civil society and government. In this workshop, representatives of civil society and government could agree or disagree with the information and conclusions of the diagnostic study presented.

4.   When the civil society representatives and government agreed on the problems, a technical, empirical study conducted by the interdisciplinary team focused on how to reduce corruption and increase efficiency in those areas (e.g., issue of permits by municipal governments) covered by the diagnostic study. The technical study identified mechanisms to reduce corruption and increase efficiency/effectiveness that were later discussed, understood, and accepted by the civil society and government representatives. Here, civil society representatives were free to devise mechanisms for monitoring and implementing the reforms, with deadlines included.

5.   The success or failure of the reforms was measured some months after the implementation stage had been completed through another survey of users demanding the same public service examined in the diagnostic study. The results were then compared to the expected results previously defined as goals by civil society groups.*

---

* A variation of this approach is being applied by the World Bank Institute. For more details, see Kaufmann, Kray, and Zoida-Lobaton.

The anticorruption policy experiences in Chile, Ecuador, and Venezuela convince us that any anticorruption campaign should be based on sound multidisciplinary scientific principles applied by research practitioners and civil society. Only a multidisciplinary approach specifying methodology, data, a scientific analysis of what works and what does not work, and, finally, the implementation of a well-specified sequencing of policy steps will help establish a solid policy consensus in the fight against systemic corruption.

Earlier studies have recognized the advantages of going beyond the analysis of the impact of corruption on economic growth and investment and stressed the need to isolate the structural features that create corrupt incentives (Rose-Ackerman 1997). But only general situations within which corruption may arise have been identified in the literature. That is, there has been no rigorous analysis of the corruption-enhancing factors within specific public institutions subject to systemic corruption.

The need to develop a testable anticorruption policy to be used within the courts has been the main reason for the empirical frameworks first introduced by Buscaglia (1997) in Ecuador and Venezuela and by Buscaglia and Dakolias (1999) in Ecuador and Chile. These studies examine the yearly changes in the reports of corruption within the courts of first instance dealing with commercial cases. This work shows that specific organizational structures and behavioral patterns within the courts in these countries made them prone to the spread of systemic corrupt practices. In short, these studies conclude that the typical Latin American court provides internal organizational incentives to be corrupt.

In theory, most developing countries possess a criminal code for punishing corrupt practices and external auditing systems within the courts for monitoring case and cash flows. Even if they function properly, however, those two mechanisms would not be enough to counter the presence of systemic corruption in the interpretation and enforcement of the law. Other dimensions need to be addressed. Certain identifiable patterns in the administrative organization of the courts coupled with a high degree of legal discretion and procedural complexities allow judges and court personnel to extract additional illicit fees for services rendered. Buscaglia (1998) also finds that corrupt practices are compounded by the lack of alternative mechanisms to resolve disputes, thus giving the official court system a virtual monopoly. More specifically, according to Buscaglia (1998, 1999), corrupt practices are enhanced by (1) a high concentration of unmonitored duties falling into the hands of a small number of people in the court, such as individual judges taking on most administrative and jurisdictional roles; (2) many complex procedural steps coupled with a lack of transparency followed in the courts; (3) serious uncertainty with respect to prevailing laws, doctrines, and regulations, such as inconsistencies in court decisions due to, among other factors, the lack of a legal database and defective information systems within the courts; (4) limited options for alternative dispute resolution; and (5) the presence of organized crime, such as drug cartels, that according to Gambetta (1993) demand corrupt practices from government officials.

These factors associated with corrupt practices provide a clear guideline for public policymaking. Developing countries, including Chile, Ecuador, and Singapore, that have enacted simpler procedural codes while introducing the kinds of alternative dispute resolutions discussed above have fewer reports of court-related corruption. Moreover, Singapore and Costa Rica have shown that corruption can be reduced by (1) drafting manuals of procedures and functions that would reduce discretion and concentration in the allocation of tasks and (2) creating specialized administrative offices in matters related to court notifications, budget and personnel management, and case and cash flows. These administrative support offices, coupled with the use of procedural manuals, have decentralized administrative decision making while reducing the concentration of organizational tasks in the hands of judges (Buscaglia 1998).

CORRUPTION'S LONG-TERM IMPACT ON EFFICIENCY AND EQUITY

Some scholars have observed that official corruption generates immediate positive results for the individual citizen or organization who is *willing and able* to pay the bribe (Rosenn 1984). For example, Rose-Ackerman (1997) accepts that "payoffs to those who manage queues can be efficient since they give officials incentives both to work quickly and favor those who value their time highly." She further states that, in some restricted cases, widely accepted illegal payoffs need to be legalized. But these statements disregard the effect that present entrenched corruption has on people's perception of social equity and on long-term efficiency. The widespread effects of corruption on the overall social system always have a pernicious effect on efficiency in the long run. To understand this effect, an economic theory of ethics needs to be applied to the understanding of the long-term effects of corruption on efficiency.

According to Root (1996, 6), "Among the world's developing nations, East Asia's high performing countries stand out for their implementation of policies that limit the effects of corruption on investment." This was because people generally felt that, despite corruption—which was usually controlled or, as in Hong Kong after the establishment of the Independent Commission Against Corruption in 1974, virtually eliminated—they had a stake in society because of good educational policies, shared growth, and the like. This stake is what people in most parts of the developing world do not feel. The economic crisis that erupted in Asia in 1997 suggests that corruption and cronyism were more serious than many analysts believed, but that does not mean Asia's governance and shared growth programs were significantly less sound.

Nonetheless, during the late 1990s even the developing Asian countries were forced to pay increasing attention to corruption. One adviser to the Shanghai Academy of Social Sciences (Zhang 1999) has said that corruption has become so common in China that most officials are involved and that it has become increasingly common among businesspeople. Reportedly, more than 158,000 Chinese, mostly party members and government officials, were punished for corruption, embezzlement, and other economic crimes between 1993 and 1998, indicating both that corruption is widespread and that the government is trying to crack down on it (Wang and Wang 1998). In March 1999 the Chinese procurator-general reported to the National People's Congress that corruption was rampant among prosecutors and that, during the year just ended, charges of corruption were made in 22,700 cases involving nearly 27,000 individuals, including the former head of the national anticorruption force (Kwan 1999). Premier Zhu Rongji pledged to the Congress that the government must "strengthen law enforcement and severely punish corruption" in the course of building an "honest, diligent, pragmatic and efficient" government (Zhu 1999).

These case studies show that the average individual's perception of how equitable a social system is has a pronounced effect on her or his incentives to engage in productive activities (Root 1996; Ratliff 1999; Buscaglia 1997). Although there have been studies examining the negative impact that corruption has on the efficient allocation of resources, that work does not pay attention to the effects that corruption has on the individual's perception of how equitable a social system is. Government corruption affects the average citizen's perception of social equity and thus the productivity and efficiency of the society as a whole. Homans (1974) argues that an individual's status within a group depends on how the group members perceive the impact of his or her contribution on them and their activities. Homans further states that members of society will respond with hostility if they see one of their member's wealth increasing substantially faster than his or her contribution to society, and that anger or envy toward the individual may precipitate destructive actions. Applying Homans's framework to our analysis of corruption, a "socially unjustified" increase in the wealth of an individual who offers and/or accepts bribes violates the average citizen's notion of what constitutes an "equitable hierarchy" within society, though this sensitivity is much more highly developed in some societies and cultures than others.

Homans's theory of ethics can be applied to understanding the long-term effect of systemic government corruption on efficiency. Members of a society who are neither able nor willing to supply illicit incentives will be effectively excluded from a government service, such as courts. In this case, even though corruption may remove red tape for those who are willing and able to pay a bribe, the provision of public services becomes inequitable in the perception of all of those who do not engage in corrupt transactions and thus are excluded from the system. This sense of inequity has a long-term effect on social interaction. Systemic government corruption promotes an inequitable social system wherein the allocation of resources is perceived to be weakly correlated to rights and obligations. Buscaglia (1997) shows that a "perceived" inequitable allocation of resources hampers the incentives to generate wealth by those who are excluded from the provision of a service. The average citizen, who cannot receive a public service due to her or his inability to pay the illegal fee, ceases to demand the public good from the official system (Buscaglia 1997). On many occasions, the higher the price demanded by corrupt actors within the public sector, the more citizens are forced to seek alternative solutions outside the government sector, whether through community-based mechanisms such as neighborhood councils or through vigilantism and other socially destructive means. Hernando de Soto's account of these community-based institutions in Peru attests to the negative consequences for a country's economy of the high transaction costs of access to public services (de Soto 1989 and forthcoming).

Thus, although at first glance it seems that eliminating bureaucratic red tape by paying a bribe enhances economic efficiency, corruption benefits—perhaps—only the individual who is *able and willing* to supply the bribe. The society in general is negatively affected because of the diminishing economic productivity over time caused by the general perception that the allocation of resources is determined more by corrupt practices than by productivity. Thus, rather than oiling the productive machine, corruption denies opportunities and prospects for equality to major sectors of the population, lowers national productivity, and reduces popular commitment to the government or nation. In this environment, individuals who need public services may have to devote additional time and attention to corrupt rather than productive activities of their own so as to be able to "buy" the public services they need. Thus present corruption decreases future productivity, thereby reducing efficiency over time.

CORRUPTION AND INSTITUTIONAL INERTIA

When designing anticorruption policies within the legal and judicial domains, we must take into account not only the costs and benefits to society of eradicating corruption in general but also the changes in present and future benefits and costs as perceived by public officials whose illicit rents will tend to diminish as a result of public anticorruption policies.

Earlier studies have argued that institutional inertia in enacting reforms stems from the long-term nature of the benefits of reform—such as enhanced job opportunities and professional prestige—in the reformers' minds (Buscaglia, Ratliff, and Dakolias 1995). These benefits cannot be directly captured in the short term by potential reformers within the government. The long-term benefits can hardly compete with such short-term losses as the anticipated decrease in the state officials' access to explicit payoffs and other informal inducements. This contrast between short-term costs and long-term benefits has often blocked judicial reforms and explains why court reforms, which eventually would benefit most segments of society, are often resisted and delayed by those currently in power. Thus reform sequencing must ensure that short-term benefits for the public officers responsible for implementing the changes somehow compensate for the certain loss of rents. In turn, reform proposals generating longer term benefits to the members of the court systems need to be implemented in the later stages of the reform process (Buscaglia, Ratliff, and Dakolias 1995).

Additional factors also enhance anticorruption initiatives. Periods of institutional crisis tend to go hand in hand with a general consensus among public officials to reform the public sector. For example, within the judiciary, a public sector crisis begins at the point where backlogs, delays, and payoffs so increase the public's cost of accessing the system that they stop regarding it highly and/or even using it. When costs become too high, most people restrict their demand for court services to the point where the capacity of judges and court personnel to justify their positions and to extract illicit payments from the public is significantly diminished. It is then that court officials begin to embrace reforms more broadly if only to keep their jobs in the midst of public outcry (Buscaglia, Ratliff, and Dakolias 1995). At this point prospects are much improved for implementing deeper reforms so long as some short-term benefits such as higher salaries, institutional independence, and increased budgets are included. Examples of developing countries that have undertaken judicial reforms during a period of deep crisis in their court systems are Costa Rica, Chile, Ecuador, Hungary, and Singapore (Buscaglia 1998). In each of these cases, short-term benefits guaranteed the political support of key magistrates who were willing to discuss judicial reform proposals only after a deep crisis threatened their jobs (Buscaglia and Ratliff 1997). The benefits they received included generous early retirement packages, promotions for judges and support staff, new buildings, and expanded budgets.

To guarantee that the anticorruption reforms will last, the short-term benefits must be channeled through permanent institutional mechanisms capable of sustaining the reforms. The best institutional arrangement is one in which public sector reforms are the by-product of a consensus involving the legislatures, judiciary, bar associations, and civil society. Here of course the problem is complicated by the fact that legislatures too sometimes oppose restructuring the courts in particular—and other public institutions in general—because doing so reduces the opportunities of legislators to extract illicit rents.

To understand and neutralize institutional inertia during anticorruption reforms, future studies must identify the costs and benefits that are relevant to those who reform public sector institutions and are responsible for implementing new anticorruption policies. Then the main question to be asked in the development of any anticorruption public policy is how to generate public policies that are based on sound empirical studies that will be accepted and adopted by the public sector and civil society. This question must be answered if countries and regions are to develop an international public policy consensus in the fight against corruption.

Conclusion

This book has explored many of the links between legal and judicial reform and economic development. As market reforms are implemented around the developing world, it is becoming increasingly clear that some of the institutions needed to consolidate the role of the private sector in the economy have been neglected. Governments from Argentina to Uganda and from China to Russia have recently realized, for example, that without legal and judicial reforms, such as the ones described in this book, many of their policy initiatives lack credibility and sustainability.

Market reforms imply a redefinition of the role of the state. In general terms, the newly proposed scope for the public domain in developing countries contemplates the state as a provider of key institutions, such as well-defined property rights and enforceable contractual frameworks, needed for markets to flourish. Efficient and equitable dispute resolution mechanisms also fall among those key institutions that the state should provide. Beyond that, the state should also encourage alternative dispute resolution (ADR) channels such as private mediation and arbitration.

In this book, we have approached the law and economics of development by identifying the type of legal institutions that foster economic efficiency—through a bottom-up approach to law making, legal transplants, and legal integration. We have also discussed the type of legal procedures needed to interpret, apply, and enforce laws in an economic system based on impersonal exchange. In this area, we have defined and analyzed the factors that could contribute to more-effective public judicial sectors and how and why these should be supplemented by alternative dispute resolution mechanisms.

We have also explained how and why corruption hampers the growth of markets by distorting the clear definition of rights to assets. We review the empirical analysis of the problem and identify those factors fostering corrupt practices within the courts. For the majority of the citizens, and the country as a whole, corruption impedes the flow of domestic and foreign investment into the most productive enterprises and efficient shared national growth. We conclude that systemic corruption is one of the most serious challenges to market reforms and political stability in the developing world. Since this is so, it follows that the causes of corruption must be identified through empirical study of corrupt systems—in our case, of judicial systems—in order to reduce its presence and devise public policies that will benefit entire nations, not just elites. We believe these proposals should be incorporated, by such international institutions as the World Bank, into public sector modernization programs in developing countries.

We have also argued that constructive legal reforms would promote political stability and economic productivity by enhancing equity. The links between legal reform, efficiency, social opportunity, and equity must be pursued by policy reformers and scholars alike. Economists tend to shy away from pointing out relationships between economic efficiency and equity. But we believe that a rigorous analysis of the compatibility between equity and efficiency is possible and useful. Developing countries face social environments in which a vast proportion of their populations live under material conditions incompatible with human dignity and political, social, and economic stability. Broadening the scope of analysis is a step toward more peaceful and productive nations and, by extension, a similar world.

The law and economics of development are capable of generating productive public policymaking. The economic analysis of the law, taking into account political and social factors, can make a critical contribution to political stability and efficient and shared economic growth in developing countries.

References

Abramowitz, Moses. 1989. *Thinking about Growth*. Cambridge: Cambridge University Press.

Acevedo, Carlos. 1987. *La Historia de la Integración* (The history of integration). Quito: Editorial Troconi.

Akerlof, George A. 1970. "The Market for Lemons: Qualitative Uncertainty and the Market Mechanism." *Quarterly Journal of Economics* 84: 488–500.

Alden, Abbott. 1976. "Latin America and International Arbitration Conventions: The Quandary of Non-Ratification." *Harvard International Law Journal* 17: 131–37.

Alesina, Alberto, S. Ozler, N. Roubini, and P. Sweagel. 1992. "Political Instability and Economic Growth." NBER Working Paper no. 4173. September.

Alford, William P. 1996. "Tasseled Loafers for Barefoot Lawyers: Transformation and Tension in the World of Chinese Legal Workers." In *China's Legal Reforms*, edited by S. Lubman. Oxford: Oxford University Press.

Alford, William P. 1995. *To Steal a Book Is an Elegant Offense: Intellectual Property Law in Chinese Civilization*. Stanford: Stanford University Press.

Andvig, Jens Christopher. 1989. "Korrupsjon i Utviklingsland" (Corruption in developing countries). *Nordisk Tidsskrift for Politisk Ekonomi* 23: 51–70.

Andvig, Jens Chr., and K. Moene, 1990. "How Corruption May Corrupt." *Journal of Economic Behavior and Organization* 13: 63–76.

Arantes, Peter, E. Gellhorn, and G. Robinson. 1983. "A Theory of Legislative Delegation." *Cornell Law Review* 68: 23–56.

Axelrod, R. 1984. *The Evolution of Cooperation*. New York: Basic Books.

Axelrod, R. 1981. "The Emergence of Cooperation among Egoists." *American Political Science Review* 75: 306–18.

Backhaus, Jurgen. 1996. "An Economic Analysis of Constitutional Law." In *The Law and Economics of Development*, edited by Edgardo Buscaglia, W. Ratliff, and R. Cooter. Greenwich: JAI Press.

Baldinelli, E. 1990. *Integración Argentina-Brasil: Un Segundo Intento Crecer* (Argentine-Brazilian integration: A second attempt to grow). Buenos Aires: Instituto Para El Desarrollo de Empresarios en la Argentina (IDEA).

Bardhan, Pranab. 1989. "The New Institutional Economics and Development Theory: A Brief Critical Assessment." *World Development* 17-9: 1389–95.

Barton, John. 1997. "The Economic and Legal Context of Contemporary Technology Transfer." In *The Law and Economics of Development,* edited by Edgardo Buscaglia, W. Ratliff, and R. Cooter. Greenwich: JAI Press.

Barzel, Yoram. 1990. *Economic Analysis of Property Rights.* New York: Cambridge University Press.

Becker, Gary. 1993. "Nobel Lecture: The Economic Way of Thinking about Behavior." *Journal of Political Economy* 108: 234–67.

Becker, Gary. 1983. "A Theory of Competition among Pressure Groups for Political Influence." *Quarterly Journal of Economics* 98: 371–83.

Becker, Gary. 1976. *The Economic Approach to Human Behavior.* Chicago: University of Chicago Press.

Becker, Gary, and G. Stigler. 1974. "Law Enforcement, Malfeasance, and Compensation of Employees." *Journal of Legal Studies* 3: 1–18.

Bell, Martin, and K. Pavitt. 1993. "Technological Accumulation and Industrial Growth: Contrasts between Developed and Developing Countries." *Industrial and Corporate Change* 2, no. 2: 157–210.

Benson, Bruce L. 1984. "Rent Seeking from a Property Rights Perspective." *Southern Economic Journal* 34: 345–78.

Birch, Melissa, and C. A. Primo Braga. 1992. "Regulation in Latin America: Prospects for the 1990s." In *Texas Papers on Latin America.* Urbana-Champaign: University of Illinois.

Birdzell, L., and N. Rosenberg. 1990. *How the West Grew Rich.* New Haven: Yale University Press.

Blair, Harry, and G. Hansen. 1994. "Weighing on the Scales of Justice: Strategic Approaches for Donor Supported Rule of Law Programs." Center for Development Information and Evaluation Program and Operations Assessment Report no. 7. Washington, D.C.: USAID.

Blount, Jeb. 1996. "Hands of Steal." *Latin Trade.* November.

Brandt, Hans-Jurgen. 1991. *En Nombre de la Paz Comunal-Un Analisis de la Justicia de Paz en el Peru* (In the name of community peace—an analysis of the justice of the peace in Peru). Lima: Centro de Investigaciones Judiciales.

Brenner, Reuven. 1994. *Labyrinths of Prosperity.* Ann Arbor: University of Michigan Press.

Brunet, Edward. 1987. "Questioning the Quality of Alternative Dispute Resolution." *Tulane Law Review* 62: 1.

Burke, John. 1996. "The Economic Basis of Law as Demonstrated by the Reformation of NIS Legal Systems." *Loyola of Los Angeles International and Comparative Law Journal* 18: 207.

Burs, Ines. 1996. "A Cost Analysis of Mediation vs. the Formal System in Argentina's Family Courts." Paper presented at the Second Annual Conference of the Inter-American Law and Economics Association. Buenos Aires, 12–13 May.

Buscaglia, Edgardo. 1999. *Judicial Corruption in Developing Countries: Its Causes and Economic Consequences.* Essays in Public Policy. Stanford: Hoover Institution Press.

Buscaglia, Edgardo. 1998a. "The Comparative Advantage of Mediation in Ecuador." Washington, D.C.: U.S. Agency for International Development. Unpublished Study.

Buscaglia, Edgardo. 1998b. "An Economic Analysis of Corrupt Practices within the Judiciary in Latin America." In *Essays in Law and Economics,* edited by C. Ott and Hans Berndt Schaeffer. Norwell, Mass.: Kluwer Press.

Buscaglia, Edgardo. 1997. "Introduction." In *The Law and Economics of Development,* edited by Edgardo Buscaglia, W. Ratliff, and R. Cooter Greenwich: JAI Press.

Buscaglia, Edgardo. 1996. "Factores Económicos que Explican la Integración Legal en Latinoamérica: El Caso de MERCOSUR" (Economic factors that explain legal integration in Latin America: The case of Mercosur). In *Contribuciones, Konrad Adenauer Foundation/Stiftung.* Buenos Aires: Konrad Adenauer Foundation Press.

Buscaglia, Edgardo. 1995a. "Judicial Reform in Latin America: The Obstacles Ahead." *Journal of Latin American Affairs* 4, no. 2: 8–16.

Buscaglia, Edgardo. 1995b. "Stark Picture of Justice in Latin America." *Financial Times,* 21 March.

Buscaglia, Edgardo. 1994. "Legal and Economic Development: The Missing Links." *Journal of Inter-American Studies and World Affairs* 35, no. 4: 153–69.

Buscaglia, Edgardo. 1993. "Law, Technological Progress, and Economic Development." Working Paper no. 119, Hoover Institution International Studies, Stanford.

Buscaglia, Edgardo, and M. Dakolias. 1999. "Comparative International Study of Court Performance Indicators: A Descriptive and Analytical Account." Legal and Judicial Reform Unit Technical Paper, World Bank.

Buscaglia, Edgardo, and M. Dakolias. 1996. "A Quantitative Analysis of the Judicial Sector: The Cases of Argentina and Ecuador." World Bank Technical Paper no. 353, World Bank.

Buscaglia, Edgardo, and M. Dakolias. 1995. "Judicial Reform in Latin American Courts: Economic Efficiency vs. Institutional Inertia." Working Paper series no. 2377-06-495, Georgetown University Graduate School of Business Administration.

Buscaglia, Edgardo, and P. Domingo. 1997. "Political and Economic Impediments to Judicial Reform in Latin America." In *The Law and Economics of Development,* edited by Edgardo Buscaglia, W. Ratliff, and R. Cooter. Greenwich: JAI Press.

Buscaglia, Edgardo, and Maria Gonzalez de Asis. Forthcoming. "A Quantitative Analysis of Public Sector Corruption." *Governance Journal.*

Buscaglia, Edgardo, and J. L. Guerrero. 1997. "Benchmarking Procedural Times: A Quality Control Approach to Court Delays." *Benchmarking for Quality Management and Technology International Journal* 40, no. 2: 84–95.

Buscaglia, Edgardo, and J. L. Guerrero. 1995. "Quantitative Analysis of Counterfeiting Activities in Developing Countries in the Pre-GATT Period." *Jurimetrics Journal* 35: 221–41.

Buscaglia, Edgardo, and Clarisa Long. 1997. *U.S. Foreign Policy and Intellectual Property Rights in Latin America.* Essays in Public Policy. Stanford: Hoover Institution Press.

Buscaglia, Edgardo, and William Ratliff. 1997. "Grassroots Democracy Is Central to Arzu's Peace." *Wall Street Journal,* 31 January.

Buscaglia, Edgardo, and T. Ulen. 1997. "A Quantitative Assessment of the Efficiency of the Judicial Sector in Latin America." *International Review of Law and Economics* 17, no. 3: 63–89.

Buscaglia, Edgardo, and T. Ulen. 1994. "A Comparative Analysis of the Intellectual Property Law in Argentina within the GATT Framework." Paper presented at the annual meeting of the American Law and Economics Association, Stanford University, 13–15 May.

Buscaglia, Edgardo, W. Ratliff, and R. Cooter, eds. 1997. *The Law and Economics of Development.* Greenwich: JAI Press.

Buscaglia, Edgardo, W. Ratliff, and M. Dakolias. 1995. *Judicial Reform in Latin America: A Framework for National Development.* Essays in Public Policy. Stanford: Hoover Institution Press. Translated from "Justicia Lenta y Venal: Un Agujero Negro en América Latina: Informe Especial" (Slow and corrupt justice: A black hole in Latin America: Special report), *Vision,* (Buenos Aires) 1–15 de abril.

Business Latin America. 1993. "MERCOSUR: Uncertain Future." 5 April.

Business Software Alliance. 1998. *1997 Global Software Piracy Report.* Washington, D.C.: International Planning and Research Corp.

Business Software Alliance. 1996. *1995 Global Software Piracy Report.* Washington, D.C.: International Planning and Research Corp.

Bussani, Mauro, and U. Mattei. 1997. "Making the Other Path Efficient: Economic Analysis and Tort Law in Less Developed Countries." In *The Law and Economics of Development,* edited by E. Buscaglia, W. Ratliff, and R. Cooter. Greenwich: JAI Press.

Cadwell, Charles. 1995. "Implementing Legal Reform in Transition Economies." Paper presented at the American Law and Economics Association annual meeting at the University of California, Berkeley, 13–14 May.

Calabresi, Guido. 1961. "Some Thoughts on Risk Distribution and the Law of Torts." *Yale Law Journal* 70: 35–46.

Campos, José Edgardo, and H. Root. 1996. *The Key to the Asian Miracle: Making Shared Growth Credible.* Washington, D.C.: Brookings Institution.

Cappelletti, Mauro. 1989. *The Judicial Process in Comparative Perspective.* Oxford: Clarendon Press.

Cappelletti, Mauro, and B. Garth. 1978. *Access to Justice: A World Survey.* Washington, D.C.: World Bank.

Carbonetto, Daniel, J. Hoyle, and M. Tueros. 1988. *Lima: Sector Informal I* (Lima: Informal sector I). Lima: Centros de Estudios para el Desarrollo y la Participación (CEDEP).

Carino, Ledivina, V., ed. 1986. *Bureaucratic Corruption in Asia: Causes, Consequences, and Controls.* Quezon City: JMC Press.

Carvalho, Jose L. 1994. *Private Sector Development and Property Rights in Latin America.* Washington, D.C.: World Bank, Latin American Technical Department.

Chudnovsky, Larry. 1992. *The Future of Hemispheric Integration: The Mercosur and the Enterprise for the Americas Initiative.* Buenos Aires: Centro de Investigaciones para la Transformación.

Clagett, Helen. 1952. *The Administration of Justice in Latin America.* Dobbs-Ferry, N.Y.: Oceana Publications.

Coase, Ronald. 1991. "The Institutional Structure of Production." In *Essays on Economics and Economists,* edited by R. Coase. Chicago: University of Chicago Press.

Coase, Ronald. 1960. "The Problem of Social Cost." *Journal of Law and Economics* 3, no. 1: 34–43.

Confucius B.C. 1923. "The Analects." In *The Four Books,* edited by James Legge. Taipei: Culture Publishers.

Consumer Protection in Brazil. 1990. Sao Paolo: Advogados.

Consumer Protection Law in India. 1991. Bombay: Tripathi Pvt. Ltd.

Cooter, Robert. 1996a. "Decentralized Law for a Complex Economy: The Structural Approach to Adjudicating the New Law Merchant." *University of Pennsylvania Law Review* 21: 129–45.

Cooter, Robert. 1996b. "The Theory of Market Modernization of Law." *International Review of Law and Economics* 16: 141–72.

Cooter, Robert. 1994. "Structural Adjudication and the New Law Merchant: A Model of Decentralized Law." *International Review of Law and Economics* 14: 215–31.

Cooter, Robert. 1991. "Inventing Market Property: The Land Courts of Papua New Guinea." *Law and Society Review* 25: 759–801.

Cooter, Robert. 1989. "The Best Right Laws: Value Foundations of the Economic Analysis of Law." *Notre Dame Law Review* 64, no. 5: 816–19.

Cooter, Robert, and T. Ginsburg. 1996. "Comparative Judicial Discretion: An Empirical Test of Economic Models." Working Paper no. 95-1, Program in Law and Economics, School of Law, University of California, Berkeley.

Cooter, Robert, and J. Gorley. 1991. "Economic Analysis in Civil Law Countries: Past, Present, Future." Symposium. *International Review of Law and Economics* 11: 261–78.

Cooter, Robert, and L. Kornhauser. 1980. "Can Litigation Improve the Law without the Help of Judges." *Journal of Legal Studies* 9: 139.

Cooter, Robert, and T. Ulen. 1988. *Law and Economics.* London: Harper Collins Publishers.

Cowell, Frank A. 1990. *Cheating the Government: The Economics of Evasion.* Cambridge: MIT Press.

Davey, William, J. Jackson, and A. Sykes. 1995. *Legal Problems of International Economic Relations.* Cambridge: Harvard University Press.

David, Rene, and J.E.C. Brierley. 1985. *Major Legal Systems in the World Today,* 3d ed. New York: Free Press.

Dakolias, Maria. 1995. "A Strategy for Judicial Reform: The Experience of Latin America." *Virginia Journal of International Law,* 36, no. 1: 167–231.

Dawson, John P. 1968. *The Oracles of the Law.* Ann Arbor: University of Michigan Law School.

de Meza, David, and J. R. Gould. 1992. "The Social Efficiency of Private Decisions to Enforce Property Rights." *Journal of Political Economy* 100: 561–80.

Deng Xiaoping. 1993. *On the Question of Hong Kong*. Beijing: Foreign Languages Press.

de Soto, Hernando. Forthcoming. *The Mystery of Capital*. New York: Basic Books.

de Soto, Hernando. 1997. Preface to *The Law and Economics of Development*, edited by Buscaglia, Ratliff, and Cooter. Greenwich: JAI Press.

de Soto, Hernando. 1989. *The Other Path*. New York: Harper and Row.

Development Associates. 1993. *Democracy Program Evaluation Report*. Washington, D.C.: Development Associates.

Dezalay, Yves, and B. Garth. 1995. "Merchants of Law as Mortal Entrepreneurs: Constructing International Justice from the Competition for Transnational Business Disputes." *Law and Society Review* 29: 27–64.

Dolinger, Jacod, and K. Rosen. 1992. *A Panorama of Brazilian Law*. Miami: North-South Center and Editora Explanada Ltd.

Dougherty, J., and L. Pfaltzgraff, Jr. 1990. *Contending Theories in International Relations*, 3d ed. New York: Harper and Row.

Douglas, Mary. 1986. *How Institutions Think*. Syracuse: Syracuse University Press.

Edwards, Harry. 1986. "Commentary: Alternative Dispute Resolution: Panacea or Anathema?" *Harvard Law Review* 99, no. 668: 45–71.

Eggertson, Thrain. 1990. *Economic Behavior and Institutions*. New York: Cambridge University Press.

Eisenberg, Melvin. 1988. *The Nature of the Common Law*. Cambridge: Harvard University Press.

Elliott, Donald, B. Ackerman, and J. Millian. 1985. "Toward a Theory of Statutory Evolution: The Federalization of Environmental Law." *Journal of Law, Economics, and Organization* 1: 313–40.

Emiola, Akintude. 1987. *Nigerian Labor Law*, 2d ed. Ethiopia: Ethiope Publishing Co.

Epstein, Edward J. 1994. "Law and Legitimation in Post-Mao China." In *Domestic Law Reforms in Post-Mao China*, edited by Pitman B. Potter. Armonk: M. E. Sharpe.

Farber, Daniel A., and P. P. Frickley. 1991. *Law and Public Choice: A Critical Introduction*. Chicago: University of Chicago Press.

Feinerman, James V. 1994. "Legal Institution, Administrative Device, or Foreign Import: The Roles of Contract in the People's Republic of China." In *Domestic Law Reforms in Post-Mao China*, edited by Pitman B. Potter. Armonk: M. E. Sharpe.

Fiorina, M. 1982. "Legislative Choice of Regulatory Forms: Legal Process or Administrative Process?" *Public Choice* 39: 33.

Fleisig, Heywood. 1994. *Law, Legal Procedure, and the Economic Value of Collateral: The Case of Bolivia*. Washington, D.C.: World Bank.

Foray, Dominique, and C. Freeman, eds. 1993. *Technology and the Wealth of Nations*. Stanford: Stanford University Press.

Galanter, Michael. 1974. "Why Haves Come Out Ahead: Speculation on the Limits of Legal Change." *Law and Society Review* 9, no. 95: 45–91.

Gambetta, Diego. 1993. *The Sicilian Mafia*. Cambridge: Harvard University Press.

Garland, David. 1990. *Punishment in Modern Society: A Study in Social Theory*. Chicago: University of Chicago Press.

General Accounting Office. 1987. *International Trade: Strengthening Worldwide Protection of Intellectual Property Rights*. Washington, D.C.: U.S. General Accounting Office.

Gil Diaz, Francisco, and A. Fernandez. 1991. "Del Desarrollo Institucional al progreso Económico" (From institutional development to economic progress). In *El Efecto de la Regulación en Algunos de los Sectores de la Economia Mexican* (The effects of regulation on some sectors of the Mexican economy), edited by Francisco Gil Diaz and A. Fernandez. Mexico City: Fondo de Cultura Económica/Instituto Tecnológico Autónomo de México.

Giraldo, Angel Jaime. 1995. *Mecanismos Alternativos para la Solución de Conflictos* (Alternative dispute resolution mechanisms). Bogota: Coyuntura Social.

Goldsmith, Jean-Claude. 1993. "ICC Working Group Report on ADR." *American Review of International Arbitration* 4, no. 4: 341–401.

Gomez Plasett, Tomas. 1989. *Debates en los Congresos Latinoamericanos*. Caracas: Editorial Bolívar.

Goodman, M. 1978. "An Economic Theory of the Evolution of the Common Law." *Journal of Legal Studies* 7, no. 393: 12–39.

Gould, David J. 1980. *Bureaucratic Corruption and Underdevelopment in the Third World: The Case of Zaire*. New York: Pergamon Press.

Gould, David J., and J. A. Amaro Reyes. 1983. "The Effects of Corruption on Administrative Performance: Illustrations from Developing Countries." Staff Working Paper No. 580, World Bank.

Granado, Juan Javier del. 1996. *Legis Imperium*. La Paz: Fondo Editorial de la Universidad Iberoamericana.

Guasch, Luis, and Pablo P. Spiller. 1994. *Regulation and Private Sector Development in Latin America*. Washingtion, D.C.: World Bank, Latin American Technical Department.

Hachette, Dominique, and R. Luders. 1993. *Privatization in Chile: An Economic Analysis*. San Francisco: ICS Press.

Hansmann, Henry, and U. Mattei. 1994. "The Comparative Law and Economics of Trusts." Paper presented at Comparative Law and Economics Foundation, Geneva.

Harrison, Lawrence. 1997. *The Pan-American Dream*. New York: Basic Books.

Harrison, Lawrence. 1985. *Underdevelopment is a State of Mind*. Lanham, Md.: University Press of America.

Hayek, Friedrich. 1973. *Law, Legislation, and Liberty*. Chicago: University of Chicago Press.

He Sheng. 1998. "Courts Face Hurdles in Backlog." *China Daily* (Beijing), 30 November.

Hirshleifer, Jack. 1982. "Evolutionary Models in Law and Economics." In *Research in Law and Economics*, edited by R.O. Zerbe. Greenwich: JAI Press.

Hirshleifer, Jack, and J. C. Coll Martinez. 1988. "What Strategies Can Support the Evolutionary Emergence of Cooperation?" *Journal of Conflict Resolution* 32: 367–98.

Hirst, M. 1988. *MERCOSUR: El Largo Camino de la Integración*. Buenos Aires: Legasa.

Homans, George C. 1974. *Social Behavior: Its Elementary Forms*. New York: Harcourt Brace Jovanovich.

Houseman, Alan W. 1993. "ADR, Justice, and the Poor." *National Institute for Dispute Resolution*, summer–fall: 56–78.

Huanca Ayaviri, Felix. 1995. *Análisis Económico del Derecho*. La Paz: Fondo Editorial de la Universidad Iberoamericana.

Huntington, Samuel. 1979. "Modernization and Corruption." In *Bureaucratic Corruption in Sub-Saharan Africa: Towards a Search for Causes and Consequences*, edited by Monday U. Ekpo. Washington, D.C.: University Press of America.

Inman, Richard. 1990. *Markets, Government, and the "New" Political Economy*. Cambridge: MIT Press.

Ippolito, Carol. 1990. "Power Balancing in Mediation: Outcomes and Implications of Mediator Intervention." *International Journal of Conflict Management* 1, no. 4: 32–71.

James, Rudolph William. 1973. *Modern Land Law in Nigeria*. Ile-Ife: University of Ife Press.

Johnson, Ian. 1999. "Class-Action Suits Let the Aggrieved in China Appeal for Rule of Law." *Wall Street Journal,* 25 March.

Johnson, Kirk. 1993. "Public Judges as Private Contractors: A Legal Frontier." *New York Times,* 10 December.

Karst, Kenneth L. 1966. *Latin American Legal Institutions: Problems for Comparative Study*. Los Angeles: UCLA Latin American Center.

Karst, Kenneth, and K. Rosen. 1975. *Law and Development in Latin America*. Berkeley: University of California Press.

Kaufmann, Daniel, Aart Kray, and Pablo Zoido-Lobaton. 1999. "Aggregating Governance Indicators." Policy Research Working Paper 2195. Washington, D.C.: World Bank.

Kikeri, Sunita, J. Nellis, and M. Shirley. 1992. *Privatization: The Lessons of Experience*. Washington, D.C.: World Bank.

Kirchner, Christian. 1991. "The Difficult Reception of Law and Economics in Germany." *International Review of Law and Economics* 11, no. 277: 277–96.

Kitch, Edmund. 1983. "Intellectual Foundations of Law and Economics." *Journal of Legal Education* 33, no. 2: 183–209.

Klitgaard, Robert. 1991. *Adjusting to Reality: Beyond State versus Market in Economic Development*. San Francisco: ICS Press.

Klitgaard, Robert. 1988. *Controlling Corruption*. Berkeley: University of California Press.

Kornhauser, Lewis A. 1984. "The Great Image of Authority." *Stanford Law Journal* 36: 349–89.

Krugman, Paul. 1993. "The Move towards Free Trade Zones." In *Policy Implications of Trade and Currency Zones*, edited by Paul Krugman. Kansas City: Federal Reserve Bank.

Kwan, Daniel. 1999. "'Rampant Corruption' among Prosecutors." *South China Morning Post,* 10 March.

L & L Law. 1998. "Debt Collection in China." Online policy statement of L & L Law Firm, China.

Lam, Willy Wo-lap. 1999. "Potholes along the Road to Change." *South China Morning Post,* 24 February.

Leff, Arthur A. 1974. "Economic Analysis of Law: Some Realism about Nominalism." *Virginia Law Review* 60, no. 78: 78–91.

Leiken, Robert S. 1996. "Controlling the Global Corruption Epidemic." *Foreign Policy* 5: 55–73.

Leoni, Bruno. 1991. *Freedom and the Law.* Indianapolis: Liberty Fund.

Libecap, Gary. "Property Rights in Economic History: Implications for Research." *Explorations in Economic History* 23, no. 3.

Long, Clarisa, and E. Buscaglia. 1997. "A Quantitative Analysis of the Legal and Economic Integration in Latin America." In *The Law and Economics of Development,* edited by E. Buscaglia, W. Ratliff, and R. Cooter. Greenwich: JAI Press.

Lubman, Stanley. 1999. *Bird in a Cage.* Stanford: Stanford University Press.

Lubman, Stanley. 1997. "There's No Rushing China's Slow March to the Rule of Law." *Los Angeles Times,* 19 October.

Lubman, Stanley. 1996a. *China's Legal Reforms.* Oxford: Oxford University Press.

Lubman, Stanley. 1996b. "Introduction: The Future of Chinese Law." In *China's Legal Reforms,* edited by S. Lubman. Oxford: Oxford University Press.

Lubman, Stanley. 1993. "International Commercial Dispute Resolution in China: A Practical Assessment." *American Review of International Arbitration* 4, no. 2: 3–18.

Lucas, Robert E. 1988. "On the Mechanics of Economic Development." *Journal of Monetary Economics* 22: 248–57.

Macrae, J. 1982. "Underdevelopment and the Economics of Corruption: A Game Theory Approach." *World Development* 10, no. 8: 677–87.

Makgetla, Neva, and R. B. Seidman. 1989. "The Applicability of Law and Economics to Policymaking in the Third World." *Journal of Economic Issues* 23, no. 1: 35–77.

Malloy, Robin. 1986. "Equating Human Rights and Property Rights: The Need for a Moral Judgment in an Economic Analysis of Law and Social Policy." *Ohio State Law Journal* 163: 78–89.

Mansfield, Edwin. 1994. "Intellectual Property Protection, Foreign Direct Investment, and Technology Transfer." Discussion Paper no. 19, International Finance Corporation, World Bank.

Marasinghe, M. L. 1984. "Towards a Third World Perspective of Jurisprudence." In *Essays on Third World Perspectives in Jurisprudence,* edited by M. L. Marasinghe and W. E. Conklin. Singapore: Malaysian Law Journal.

Margadant, Guillermo Floris. 1983. *An Introduction to the History of Mexican Law.* Dobbs-Ferry, N.Y.: Oceana Publications.

Martinelli, Cesar, and M. Tommasi. 1997. "Sequencing of Economic Reforms in the Presence of Political Constraints." *Economics and Politics* 9, no. 2: 115–31.

Martinez, Gabriel. 1997. "Competition Policy and Deregulation in Mexico in the late 1990s." In *The Law and Economics of Development*, edited by E. Buscaglia, W. Ratliff, and R. Cooter. Greenwich: JAI Press.

Mathews, R. C. O. 1986. "The Economics of Institutions and the Source of Growth." *Economic Journal* 69: 89–105.

Mattei, Ugo. 1994. "Efficiency in Legal Transplants: An Essay in Comparative Law and Economics." *International Review of Law and Economics* 14: 13–93.

Mattei, Ugo. 1993. "Law and Economics in Civil Law Countries: A Comparative Approach." *International Review of Law and Economics* 14, no. 3: 265–75.

Mattick, Ross. 1992. "Agrarian Reform in West Bengal: The End of an Illusion." *World Development* 20, no. 5: 735–50.

Mauro, Paolo. 1995. "Corruption and Growth." *Quarterly Journal of Economics* III: 681–711.

McKinnon, Ronald. 1991. *Lessons of Economic Liberalization: Financial Control in the Transition to a Market Economy*. Baltimore: Johns Hopkins University Press.

McKinnon, Ronald. 1982. "The Order of Economic Liberalization: Lessons from Chile and Argentina." In *Economic Policy in a World of Change*, edited by K. Brunner and A. Metzler. Amsterdam: North Holland.

McQuillan, Lawrence J., and P. C. Montgomery. 1999. *The International Monetary Fund: Financial Medic to the World?* Stanford: Hoover Institution Press.

Meese, Edwin. 1999. "The Dangerous Federalization of Crime." *Wall Street Journal*, 22 February.

Mercuro, Nicholas, and T. P. Ryan. 1984. *Law, Economics, and Public Policy*. Greenwich: JAI Press.

Merryman, John Henry. 1985. *The Civil Law Tradition*. Stanford: Stanford University Press.

Merryman, John Henry, and D. Clark. 1978. *Comparative Law: Western European and Latin American Legal Systems: Cases and Materials*. Indianapolis: Bobbs-Merrill.

Milgrom, Paul, and J. Roberts. 1988. "An Economic Approach to Influence Activities in Organizations." *American Journal of Sociology* 94, supplement: 45–90.

MLW. 1992. "The Privatization of Justice." *Massachusetts Lawyers Weekly*, 22 June: 35–47.

Mols, M. 1993. "The Integration Agenda: A Framework for Comparison." In *The Challenge of Integration: Europe and the Americas*, edited by Peter H. Smith. Coral Gables: University of Miami North South Center.

Myrdal, Gunnar. 1989. "Corruption as a Hindrance to Modernization in South Asia." In *Political Corruption: A Handbook*, edited by A. J. Heidenheimer, M. Johnson, and V. Le Vine. New Brunswick: Transactions Publishers.

Nadelmann, Ethan A. 1993. *Cops across Borders: The Internationalization of U.S. Criminal Law Enforcement*. University Park: Pennsylvania State Press.

National Center for State Courts. 1994. "First Inter-American Meeting on Alternative Dispute Resolution: Final Report." In *Report from the Annual Meeting*, Buenos Aires, 7–10 November.

National Council. 1998. *Republic of Argentina*. Buenos Aires: Justicialista Party.

Nofal, M. 1993. *Economic Integration of Argentina-Brazil, MERCOSUR, and Regionalization in the Southern Cone Market*. Buenos Aires: Nofal y Asociados.

North, Douglass. 1991. "Institutions." *Journal of Economic Perspectives* 5, no. 1: 3–17.

North, Douglass. 1990. *Institutions, Institutional Change, and Economic Performance*. Cambridge: Cambridge University Press.

North, Douglass. 1987. "Institutions, Transaction Costs, and Economic Growth." *Economic Inquiry* 25: 456–89.

North, Douglass. 1981. *Structure and Change in Economic History*. New York: W. W. Norton.

North, Douglass, and B. Weingast. 1989. "The Evolution of Institutions Governing Public Choice in 17th Century England." *Journal of Economic History* 49: 803–32.

Nozick, Robert. 1974. *Anarchy, State and Utopia*. New York: Basic Books.

Ogus, Anthony. 1995. "Economics and Law Reform: Thirty Years of Law Commission Endeavor." *Law Quarterly Review* 111: 407–20.

O'Hare, Judith. 1996. "Arbitration and Alternative Dispute Resolution: A Hong Kong Perspective." *American Review of International Arbitration* 7, no. 1: 14–24.

Olson, Mancur. 1993. "Dictatorship, Democracy, and Development." *American Political Science Review* 87: 567–76.

Olson, Mancur. 1982. *The Rise and Decline of Nations*. New Haven: Yale University Press.

Olson, Mancur. 1965. *The Logic of Collective Action: Public Goods and the Theory of Groups*. Cambridge: Harvard University Press.

Omnibus Trade and Competitiveness Act of 1988, 19. 1301-1303 (amending Section 301 of the Trade Act of 1974 to include a "Special 301" to deal with intellectual property protection).

Orr, Daniel, and T. Ulen. 1993. "The Role of Trust and the Law in Privatization." *Quarterly Review of Economics and Finance* 33 (special issue): 135–55.

Ostrom, Elnor. 1990. *Governing the Commons: The Evolution of Institutions for Collective Action*. Cambridge: Cambridge University Press.

Ott, Claus, and H-B. Schafer. 1991. "Emergence and Construction of Efficient Rules in the Legal System of German Civil Law." Paper presented at the European Law and Economics Association.

Paredes, Ricardo. 1997. "Jurisprudence of the Antitrust Commissions in Chile." In *The Law and Economics of Development*, edited by E. Buscaglia, W. Ratliff, and R. Cooter. Greenwich: JAI Press.

Pastor, Santos. 1991. "Informe sobre la Litigación, Recursos, y Acceso de los Ciudadanos a la Justicia"(Report on litigation, resources, and access of citizens to justice). In *Materiales para una Reforma Procesal* (Materials for a reform of the procedural code). Madrid: Ministerio de Justicia.

Pastor, Santos. 1989. *Economia y Sistema Jurídico: Una Introducción al Análisis Económico del Derecho* (Economics and legal system: An introduction to economic analysis of the law). Madrid: Tecnos.

Paz, Octavio. 1994. "Reflections: Mexico and the United States." In *A New Moment in the Americas,* edited by Robert Leiken. New Brunswick: Transaction Publishers.

Pearl, Daniel. 1996. "Big Drug Makers Push Egypt, Other Nations to End Their 'Piracy.'" *Wall Street Journal,* 13 December.

Pharmaceutical Research Association. 1996. *Opportunities and Challenges for Pharmaceutical Innovation.* Washington, D.C.: Congressional Research Service.

Porter, Michael. 1985. *Competitive Advantage.* New York: Free Press.

Posner, Richard. 1992. "The Federal Courts: Crisis and Reform." In *Economic Analysis of Law.* Boston: Little Brown.

Posner, Richard. 1980. "A Theory of Primitive Society, with Special Reference to Law." *Journal of Law and Economics* 23: 1–25.

Potter, Pitman B. 1996. "Foreign Investment Laws in the People's Republic of China: Dilemmas of State Control." In *China's Legal Reforms,* edited by S. Lubman. Oxford: Oxford University Press.

Potter, Pitman B. 1995. *Foreign Business Law in China: Past Progress and Future Challenges.* San Francisco: The 1990 Institute.

Potter, Pitman B. 1994. *Domestic Law Reforms in Post-Mao China.* Armonk: M. E. Sharpe.

Prebisch, Raúl. 1950. *The Economic Development of Latin America and Its Principal Problems.* Lake Success, N.Y.: United Nations.

Priest, George L. 1987. "Measuring Legal Change." *Journal of Law, Economics, and Organization* 3: 193–225.

Primo Braga, Carlos. 1990. "The Developing Country Case for or against Intellectual Property Protection." In *Strengthening Protection of Intellectual Property in Developing Countries.* Washington, D.C.: World Bank.

Ramseyer, J. Mark. 1989. "Water Law in Imperial Japan: Public Goods, Private Claims, and Legal Convergence." *Journal of Legal Studies* 51: 310–41.

Ramseyer, J. Mark, and F. M. Rosenbluth. 1995. *The Politics of Oligarchy: Institutional Choice in Imperial Japan.* New York: Cambridge University Press.

Ratliff, William. 1999. "Development and Civil Society in Latin America and Asia." *Annals of the American Academy of Political and Social Science,* fall: 91–112.

Ratliff, William. 1998. "Bending the Law in Latin America." *Policy Studies Review* 15, nos. 2/3: 126–43.

Ratliff, William. 1997. "Judicial Reform: The Neglected Priority in Latin America." *Annals of the American Academy of Political and Social Science* 550: 59–71.

Ratliff, William. 1996. "Libertades Civiles e Inversión Privada" (Civil liberties and private investment). *Vision* (Buenos Aires), 1–15 de abril.

Ratliff, William. 1992. "Latins Take on the U.S. Supreme Court." *Wall Street Journal,* 3 July.

Ratliff, William. 1989–90. "Latin American Studies: Up from Radicalism?" *Academic Questions* 3, no. 1: 60–74.

Ratliff, William, and E. Buscaglia. 1997. "Judicial Reform: Institutionalizing Change in the Americas." In *Law and Economics of Development,* edited by E. Buscaglia, W. Ratliff, and R. Cooter. Greenwich: JAI Press.

Ratliff, William, and R. Fontaine. 1993. *Argentina's Capitalist Revolution Revisited: Confronting the Social Costs of Statist Mistakes.* Essay in Public Policy. Stanford: Hoover Institution Press.

Ratliff, William, and R. Fontaine. 1990. *Changing Course: The Capitalist Revolution in Argentina.* Essays in Public Policy. Stanford: Hoover Institution Press.

Rawls, John. 1971. *A Theory of Justice.* Cambridge: Harvard University Press.

Report of the United States Trade Representative's Intergovernmental Policy Advisory Committee (IGPAC) to the Congress of the United States on the Agreements Reached in the Uruguay Round of Multilateral Trade Negotiations, 14 January 1994, p. 22.

Restivo, Nestor. 1997. "EE UU Sancionaría hoy a la Argentina por las Patentes" (The United States applies santions to Argentina due to its patent system). *Clarín* (Buenos Aires), 14 January.

Reuven, Brenner. 1980. "Economics: An Imperialistic Science?" *Journal of Legal Studies* 9, no. 1: 12–21.

Roemer, Andrés. 1993. *Introducción al Análisis Económico del Derecho* (An introduction to the economic analysis of the law). Mexico City: Fondo de Cultura Económica.

Roemer, Andrés. 1989. *Evaluación Jurídica, Financiera, y Económica de la Camaronicultura en México* (Legal, financial, and economic evaluation of the shrimp industry in Mexico). Mexico City: Instituto Tecnológico Autónomo de México.

Root, Hilton. 1996. *Small Countries, Big Lessons: Governance and the Rise of East Asia.* Hong Kong: Oxford University Press.

Root, Hilton, W. Ratliff, and A. Morgan. Forthcoming. "What Latin America Can Learn from Asia's Development Experience." In *Critical Issues for Mexico and the Developing World,* edited by Kenneth Judd. Stanford: Hoover Institution Press.

Rose-Ackerman, Susan. 1997. "Corruption and Development." Unpublished manuscript.

Rose-Ackerman, Susan. 1986. "Reforming Public Bureaucracy through Economic Incentives?" *Journal of Law, Economics, and Organization* 2, no. 1: 1–19.

Rose-Ackerman, Susan. 1981. "Does Federalism Matter: Political Choice in a Federal Republic." *Journal of Political Economy* 89: 89–93.

Rose-Ackerman, Susan. 1980. "Risk-Taking and Reelection: Does Federalism Promote Innovation?" *Journal of Legal Studies* 89: 12–38.

Rose-Ackerman, Susan. 1978. *Corruption: A Study in Political Economy.* New York: Academic Press.

Rosenn, Keith S. 1984. "Brazil's Legal Culture: The Jeto Revisited." *Florida International Law Journal* 5 (fall): 23–41.

Rubin, Edward. 1996. "The New Legal Process: The Synthesis of Discourse and the Microanalysis of Institutions." Commentary in *Harvard Law Review* 109: 1393.

Rubin, Paul. 1993. "Growing a Legal System, with Special Reference to the Post-Communist Economies." Working Paper no. 63, Center for International Reform and the Informal Sector.

Saharay, H. K. 1988. *Labor and Social Laws in India.* Vol. 5, 34–45. Eastern Law House.

Santhanam Committee, Ministry of Home Affairs, 1994. Report by the Committee on Prevention of Corruption, Government of India.

Schlesinger, Rudolf B. 1959. "Common Law and Civil Law-Comparison of Methods and Sources." In *Comparative Law: Cases, Texts, and Materials.* Brooklyn: Foundation Press.

Seidman, Ann, and R. Seidman. 1996. "Drafting Legislation for Development: Lessons from a Chinese Project." *American Journal of Comparative Law* 44, no. 1: 1–16.

Seidman, Robert B. 1978. *State, Law, and Development.* New York: St. Martin's Press.

Shleifer, Andrei. 1994. "Establishing Property Rights." In *Proceedings of the World Bank at the Annual Conference.* Washington D.C.: World Bank.

Shleifer, Andrei, and R. Vishny. 1993. "Corruption." *Quarterly Journal of Economics* 10: 599–617.

Simpson, A. W. B. 1975. *A History of Common Law of Contract.* Oxford: Clarendon Press.

Smith, Adam. 1978. *Lectures on Jurisprudence.* Oxford: Oxford University Press.

Smith, Peter. 1993. "The Politics of Integration: Concepts and Themes." In *The Challenge of Integration: Europe and the Americas,* edited by Peter H. Smith. Coral Gables: University of Miami North South Center.

Snidal D. 1991. "Relative Gains and International Cooperation." *American Political Science Review* 85, no. 4: 1303–20.

Spain, Larry. 1994. "Alternative Dispute Resolution for the Poor: Is It an Alternative?" *North Dakota Law Review* 70, no. 269: 270–99.

Stokes, Bruce. 1997. "The Chinese Challenge." *Financial Times,* April 12.

Stone, Andrew, B. Levy, and R. Paredes. 1992. "Public Institutions and Private Transactions: The Legal and Regulatory Environment for Business Transactions in Brazil and Chile." Policy Research Working Paper series 891, World Bank.

Terrell, Timothy. 1987. "Rights and Wrongs in the Rush to Repose: On the Jurisprudential Dangers of Alternative Dispute Resolution." *Emory Law Journal* 36, no. 54: 541–56.

Tokman, Victor. 1992. *Beyond Regulation: The Informal Economy in Latin America.* Boulder: Lynne Rienner.

Tokman, Victor. 1989. "Policies for a Heterogeneous Informal Sector in Latin America." *World Development* 17: 1067–76.

Trebilcock, Michael. 1997. "What Makes Poor Countries Poor? The Role of Institutional Capital in Economic Development." In *The Law and Economics of Development,* edited by E. Buscaglia, W. Ratliff, and R. Cooter. Greenwich: JAI Press.

Trebilcock, Michael. 1983. "The Prospects of Law and Economics: A Canadian Perspective." *Journal of Legal Education* 33: 288–90.

Trubek, E. 1972. "Towards a Social Theory of Law: An Essay on the Study of Law and Development." *Yale Law Journal* 82, no. 1: 1–18.

Ulen, Thomas. 1997. "Law's Contributions to Economic Growth." In *The Law and Economics of Development,* edited by E. Buscaglia, W. Ratliff, and R. Cooter. Greenwich: JAI Press.

United States Embassy, Beijing. 1995a. "Protecting Intellectual Property: Developing Country Issues," 29 June.

United States Embassy, Beijing. 1995b. "USTR Fact Sheet on U.S.-China IPR Agreement," 2 March.

Uvieshara, E. E. 1976. *Trade Union Law in Nigeria.* Benin City: Ethiope Publishing Company.

van den Bergh, Roger. 1992. "Law and Economics in Europe: Present State and Future Prospects." In *Bibliography of Law and Economics,* edited by B. Bouckaert and G. de Geest. Boston: Kluwer Academic.

van Klaveren, Alberto. 1993. "Why Integration Now? Options for Latin America." In *The Challenge of Integration: Europe and the Americas,* edited by Peter H. Smith. Coral Gables: University of Miami North South Center.

Velez Muniz, Ricardo. 1951. *El Acercamiento de los Sistemas Legales en Latinoamérica* (The convergence of legal systems in Latin America). Buenos Aires: Editorial UBA.

Wang Yong, and Wang Chuandong. 1998. "Party Set to Stamp out Corruption." *China Daily,* 13 March.

Watson, Alan. 1983. *The Civil Law.* Cambridge: Cambridge University Press.

Watson, Alan. 1978a. *Society and Legal Change.* Cambridge: Cambridge University Press.

Watson, Alan. 1978b. "Comparative Law and Legal Change." *Columbia Law Journal* 313: 45–67.

Watson, Alan. 1974. *Legal Transplants: An Approach to Comparative Law.* Cambridge: Harvard University Press.

White, Eduardo. 1975. *Control of Restrictive Practices in Latin America.* New York: Viking Press.

Williamson, Oliver. 1991. "Intellectual Foundations: The Need for a Broader View." *Journal of Legal Education* 33, no. 2: 210–16.

Wilson, James Q. 1989. *Bureaucracy: What Government Agencies Do and Why They Do It.* New York: Basic Books.

Winn, Jane Kaufman. 1994. "Not by Rule of Law: Mediating State-Society Relations in Taiwan through the Underground Economy." In *The Other Taiwan: 1945 to the Present,* edited by Murray Rubinstein. London: M. E. Sharpe.

World Bank. 1997. *World Development Report 1997.* Oxford: Oxford University Press.

World Bank. 1993. "Ecuador: Constraints to Private Sector Development." Trade, Finance, and Private Sector Development Division, Washington, D.C.

World Economic Forum. 1993 and 1994. *World Competitiveness Report.* Baltimore: Johns Hopkins University.

Zhang Zhongli. 1999. "Laws Urged to Tackle Corruption." *Hong Kong Standard,* 9 March.

Zhu Rongji. 1999. "Premier Spells Out Tasks to NPC." *China Daily,* 6 March.

Ziskind, David. 1987. *Labor Provisions in African Constitutions.* Los Angeles: Litlaw Foundation.

Index

ABEIP, 47–48
Administrative law, 12
ADR mechanisms, 71–86, 101;
  advantages and disadvantages of,
  75–81; common private channels,
  76–77; court-annexed channels,
  77–78; crisis generated, 74; in
  developed countries, 80; formal
  court *versus*, 79–81; for-profit
  types, 83, 84; lack of precedent and,
  85–86; need for, 83–84; public
  versus private, 81–83; use and
  scope of, 84–86
Africa, 73, 74
Agrarian economies, 37, 39, 54
Agro-manufacturing, 40–41
Alfonsín, Raúl, 47
Alfonsín-Sarney agreement, 47, 51
Alford, William, 19, 20, 68, 69
Analects, 20
Andean Pact, 34, 36
Argentina, 17, 22, 23, 34, 37, 38;
  ABEIP and, 47, 52; ADR
  mechanisms in, 76, 77, 78, 79, 84;
  Falklands/Malvinas war, 50–51;
  industrialization and legal change,
  40; judiciary in, 17, 60, 62–65, 74;
  Mercosur and, 46; overlapping
  economic structures and, 53;
  trade-driven institutional
  harmonization and, 43
Asean, 36
Asia, 2; ADR mechanisms in, 74;
  corruption in, 95; development,
  post-WWII, 3; economic blocs in,
  34, 36; equitable or shared growth
  in, 3, 9, 16, 95, 102;
  parliamentary system in, 73; trade
  agreements, 34
Automobile industry, 44, 52

Banks, 7, 90
"Best practice" standards, 17
Biotech products, 44
Bolivia, 34, 37, 40
Brand names, 38
Brazil, 23, 26, 34, 37, 38; ABEIP
  and, 47, 52; industrialization and
  legal change, 40; judiciary in, 60;
  Mercosur and, 46; overlapping
  economic structures and, 53;
  transition from military
  government, 50–51
Bribery, 94–95, 96
Buenos Aires Act (1990), 48
Bulgaria, 20
Bustamante Code, 39

Calvo Doctrine, 42
Canada, 34
Caricom, 36
Centralized lawmaking, 13, 72, 73
CEPAL, 43
Chemical industry, 26, 44
Chile, 26, 34, 38; anticorruption
  policies in, 90, 92–93, 94; FTA and,
  46; industrial and service sectors in,
  40; judiciary in, 61, 99; Napoleonic
  code and, 37
China: ADR mechanisms in, 76;
  corruption in, 95–96; cultural
  factors in, 45; dysfunctional
  judiciary in, 57, 67, 74; intellectual
  property and, 17, 19, 20, 23; legal
  reform in, 12, 22; piracy of
  property, 20; professionalism in
  judiciary, 68–69; transplants in, 15
CIDIP, 39–40
Civil law, 12, 15, 33, 38, 72
Civil service reform, 90
Class-action suits, 68

ABOUT THE AUTHORS

EDGARDO BUSCAGLIA is the director of the Law and Economics of Development Center and the vice president of the Inter-American Law and Economics Association. He is a fellow at the Hoover Institution at Stanford University and at the University of Virginia School of Law and an adviser to several international organizations in the United States and Europe. His publications focus on the law and economics of development.

WILLIAM RATLIFF is a senior research fellow and curator of the Americas Collection at the Hoover Institution. His books and articles focus on the political factors causing stagnation or promoting growth in developing countries and on U.S. foreign policy in Europe, Asia, and Latin America. He has published commentaries in all major U.S. newspapers and is a frequent contributor to MSNBC on the Internet.